Praise for North Star Habits

This is a wonderful collection of inspiring stories celebrating the power of ritual and positive habits in our lives. I gobbled up the stories, completely transported to the different circumstances and each writer's celebration of how they brought joy into their lives by trying something new. Stories are worth a thousand worthy words. The earnest theory of behaviour change becomes colourful and moving when told as a story about a real person's life. Thank you to Fleur and all the wonderful storytellers for giving us this volume. Highly recommended!
Vidyamala Burch OBE, mindfulness and compassion teacher, award-winning author and co-founder of *Breathworks*

North Star Habits is a guiding light for finding our way home to ourselves in our darkest and most challenging moments. It is a book of love, tenderness and awe, reminding us that habits can be kind, gentle and nourishing. I feel inspired and uplifted by these beautiful stories of hope.
Claire Harrison, leadership coach and meditation teacher

It's easy to lose perspective, but *North Star Habits* shows us how to find our footing again in the humblest and sometimes most hilarious ways. Seventeen distinct and dynamic tales explore how we can overcome adversity, push beyond our limits and change our paths through the simplest rituals and transformative habits. It makes you feel excited about what you may find in the bottom your next bowl of homemade soup or within the expansive ocean if you take a brave dip!
Kate Luckins PhD, author of *Live More with Less: Upgrade Your Life without Costing the Earth!*

North Star Habits is a beautifully curated collection of true stories that give insight into the ordinary actions that create extraordinary lives. Full of wisdom, warmth and raw human experiences from around the globe, it demonstrates that magic lies within all of us and can be expressed through simple, sacred moments. We learn that by acting with intention and intuition, profound healing is possible for ourselves and our societies. This book is essential reading for anyone ready to participate more fully in the flow of life.
Johanna de Burca, co-founder and CEO, *Just Peoples*

Each of us has a purpose in this beautiful world - discovering and achieving that purpose requires honesty and courage. *North Star Habits* shares beautiful stories from people around the world who have found their own personal rituals to determine, chart and embark upon their journeys, successfully aligning and intertwining life, love and work.
Lizzie Corke OAM, co-founder and CEO, *Conservation Ecology Centre* (Australia)

What a wonderfully comforting read! Each tender story made me feel less alone and reminded me that life is sweeter and more meaningful when we choose daily habits that inspire and nourish us!
Sarah Bamford Seidelmann, author of *Swimming with Elephants: My Unexpected Pilgrimage from Physician to Healer*

North Star Habits is a gorgeous collection of real-world, real-life stories to warm your heart and inspire you! Every story, every person unique and also alike in their humanness. A wonderful and uplifting read, perfect for snuggling up with a cup of tea in hand.
Karen Buckland, yoga and meditation teacher

This book is a beautiful reminder that personal transformation doesn't need to always come from the big, bold decisions. It can seed from seemingly tiny, inspired actions, taken consistently and from the heart. It is when we listen to the whisper we reap the rewards.
Vanessa Barrington, the book doula, *Healing House Publishing*

North Star Habits offers thought-provoking and often moving stories from a diverse range of people finding their way to more peaceful and meaningful lives. I'm inspired.
Rata Gordon, poet, mentor and author of *Second Person*

Thoughtful, heartfelt and enlightening experiences.
Clifford Posner, owner, *The Grumpy Swimmer* (Bookstore)

North Star Habits is a profound collection where each chapter shares a personal journey of awakening, growth and transformation. Each story reveals how becoming conscious of the unconscious habits and beliefs that keep us stuck can unlock the immeasurable power of intentionally cultivating new thoughts and beliefs to change the trajectory of our lives.
Joanna Kleinman, author of *Dethroning your Inner Critic: The Four-Step Journey from Self-Doubt to Self-Empowerment*

This book is a jewel for anyone looking for inspiration to create or reignite soulful habits. It offers seventeen personal stories with unique and fresh approaches on how value-driven habits helped them navigate adversity, and how these habits were a form of self-expression and finding a home within. This anthology is a great compilation of profound stories.
Sonee Singh, Doctor of Divinity and multi-award-winning poet and novelist

Praise for
Wholehearted Confidence

Fleur Chambers has done it again, offering soulful guidance that is fresh, helpful, deeply grounded and wise, and comes straight from the heart.
Rick Hanson PhD, psychologist and author of *Resilient: How to Grow an Unshakable Core of Calm, Strength, and Happiness*

Fleur has such a beautiful way of bringing together deep spiritual insights with practical day-to-day action – a rare gift! And her lived experience of finding confidence in her own voice is a true inspiration. This book will change you.
Amy Taylor-Kabbaz, matrescence activist and author of *Mama Rising*

A gentle paddle down the river of life with Fleur as your guide. Rest assured; you will be well looked after. Beautifully written and full of warmth and wisdom.
Andy Hobson, meditation teacher and musician

Fleur has a gift for taking tricky subjects like trauma, our shadow sides and self-worth and making them so relatable that the reader will feel empowered to make pivotal changes in their life.
Jacqui Lewis, founder of *The Broad Place* **and author of** *The 14 Day Mind Cleanse*

Praise for Ten Pathways

This heartfelt, smart and practical book will help you feel better from the very first page. Fleur Chambers has a remarkable gift for offering super-effective ideas and tools in a warm, down-to-earth, and encouraging voice. Plus, it's just beautiful. This is a gem.
Rick Hanson PhD, author of *Buddha's Brain: The Practical Neuroscience of Happiness, Love, and Wisdom*

Your go-to guide for good days, bad days and everything in-between. Fleur has an amazing ability to reframe what it means to be happy and drop her readers into gratitude. Whether you've experienced chronic pain or not, the ten pathways aren't a quick fix, but a total mindset reset. Every page delivers a big dose of healing! This book is a gift!
Amy Molloy, author of *Wife Interrupted*

Life can be painful and messy. But – according to Fleur Chambers – joy and vitality can be found in the midst of the mess. In this beautifully designed book, written with humour and wisdom, Fleur shows us how. Equal parts whimsical and sensible, reassuring and wise, it will make you feel better even if it just sits on your bedside table!
Matthew Young, director, *Melbourne Meditation Centre*

Fleur's book is a wonderful resource for anyone who is curious about how mindfulness can help with any kind of pain. Full of practical, thoughtful ideas, as well as Fleur's personal journey, this engaging and beautiful book will make you feel that you're sitting in the room with a kind and supportive friend.
Kate James, author of *Change Your Thinking to Change Your Life*

NORTH STAR HABITS

CURATED BY
FLEUR CHAMBERS

THE FLEUR CHAMBERS COLLECTION

Copyright Fleur Chambers 2024

First published in Australia in 2024
By The Fleur Chambers Collection

In the spirit of reconciliation The Fleur Chambers Collection acknowledges the Traditional Custodians of Country throughout Australia and their connections to land, sea and community. We pay our respect to their Elders past and present and extend that respect to all Aboriginal and Torres Strait Islander peoples today.

All rights reserved. Except as permitted under the Australian Copyright Act 1968 (for example, a fair dealing for the purposes of study, research, criticism or review), no part of this book may be reproduced, stored in a retrieval system, communicated or transmitted in any form or by any means without prior written permission.

All enquiries should be made to the author.

A catalogue record for this work is available from the National Library of Australia

National Library of Australia Catalogue-in-Publication data:
North Star Habits/Fleur Chambers

Cover Design by Amygdala Design
Typeset by Dylan Ingram
Editing by Amy Molloy

978-1-7636406-0-3 (Hardback)
978-1-7636406-1-0 (Paperback)
978-1-7636406-2-7 (Ebook)

Disclaimer
The material in this publication is of the nature of general comment only, and does not represent professional advice. It is not intended to provide specific guidance for particular circumstances and it should not be relied on as the basis for any decision to take action or not take action on any matter which it covers. Readers should obtain professional advice where appropriate, before making any such decision. To the maximum extent permitted by law, the author and publisher disclaim all responsibility and liability to any person, arising directly or indirectly from any person taking or not taking action based on the information in this publication.

This book is dedicated to all the people, places and moments that guided us back home.

Contents

Foreword
Habits of Hope by Amy Molloy 1

Introduction
From Routine to Ritual, Simple to Sacred by Fleur Chambers 5

Chapter One
Feeling All My Feelings by Brenda Lee Nelson 11

Chapter Two
My Escape, My Solace, My Reset by Ross Pollard 21

Chapter Three
Words From My Grandmother by Mercy Kafotokoza 31

Chapter Four
Trail Adventures of a Dog and a Hippie by Ed Jones 40

Chapter Five
Soup, Song and Self-Compassion by Jennifer Robertson 51

Chapter Six
Stop. Look. Listen. by Melanie Birtchnell 60

Chapter Seven
Saving Lives by Sal Pollard 70
Chapter Eight
Making My Own Splash by Mandy Mercuri 79
Chapter Nine
Take It Easy by Shah Rafayat Chowdhury... 90
Chapter Ten
Fear Less by Gregory Murray.. 99
Chapter Eleven
Show Me the Way by Lisa Benson... 110
Chapter Twelve
Catching the Wind by Fred Locke 120
Chapter Thirteen
Choosing Love Over Fear by Christey West 128
Chapter Fourteen
The Healing Habits of a Highly Sensitive Person by Sara Lynn Shemonsky.. 138
Chapter Fifteen
You Are Beautiful by Margie Dannenbaum....................................... 148
Chapter Sixteen
From Acorn to Oak by Tom Macior 157
Chapter Seventeen
Finding Strength in Words by Tang Duyen Hong............................ 167
Epilogue
Owning our Pivotal Moments by Fleur Chambers 176

Fourteen-Day North Star Habit Challenge 180
References 183
Acknowledgements 185

Foreword

Habits of Hope

By Amy Molloy

As a journalist and magazine editor, I have asked hundreds of interviewees this trendy question since the noughties: *What's your morning routine?* It has become somewhat of a joke in interviews with celebrities, entrepreneurs and influencers, so desperate are we to unlock the magic secret to starting our day on the right foot, in the hope that we can sidestep adversity.

What most people dislike about this question is the cookie-cutter answer: wake up at 5am, workout, meditate, drink a green smoothie, 'eat a frog' (in other words, do the item on your to-do list that you're dreading), maybe chuck in a random act of kindness.

There was a time in my life when I planned my morning, and my entire week, like this – and then I became a parent of three wild and wonderful children.

As a mother of three aged seven and under, my habits must tick three boxes: flexible, fluid and, hopefully, fulfilling. Ideally, they also satisfy two self-care categories: fitness and social connection, mental health and creativity. So, I meditate in my car after school drop-off; I play a Hertz healing playlist whilst doing Play-Doh with my three-year-old; I swim in our local rockpool because I like chatting to the elders who never miss a morning even in the depths of winter.

It's not always Instagram-worthy, but it works for our family – and, when it comes to habits, you have to be your own role model.

Saying that, we all need inspiration and hope. And that is why I jumped at the chance when Fleur asked me to be part of this project. I have been working with Fleur since I edited her first book, *Ten Pathways,* in 2021 and, every time I edit her words and wisdom, it has a knock-on effect on my personal life.

With *Ten Pathways,* it taught me to stop 'shooting the second arrow' of suffering when I face adversity. With her next book, *Wholehearted Confidence*, I discovered that my self-esteem could be strong, but also feel soft, which transformed the way I lead my family.

As for this book, *North Star Habits* … Well, I was a little worried that I'd be tasked with editing seventeen cookie-cutter answers. What I discovered, however, as I read these chapters, was just how rich and varied people's habits were. Collectively, they reminded me of two things:

1. The most powerful habits take us by surprise.
2. Your most life-changing habits are in front of you – no matter what age you are now.

As I edited the short stories that you will read in this book, I fell in love with the people you will meet in the next seventeen chapters, and I implemented some of their habits immediately. I thought of them as I swam in the ocean or as I cooked dinner for my kids. They came to mind when I criticised myself in the mirror, or on those overwhelming days as a mother when you feel like you're disappearing and draining every colour in your rainbow. Each of these authors, in different ways, gave me incredible hope and faith in myself and my future.

It's easy as we age and evolve to think we've lost many of our passions or our hobbies – and we'll never replace them. But this book is proof there is always a habit waiting for you to discover it; from a conversation with a friend, a chance meeting, a health challenge or a book like this one. The truth is: you haven't met the habits that will really transform your life yet. And that is an amazing realisation.

If you're a fan of the book *Atomic Habits* by James Clear, you'll know how important daily habits are for our health and our wellbeing, our relationships and our careers, our bank balances and our creativity. I have a James Clear quote stuck in my kitchen: *Every habit is a vote for the person you want to be.* But that person – the shiny version of ourselves we hope we'll meet if we swap our morning coffee for hot water, lemon and ginger – is always changing and evolving.

Part of the secret is to hold your habits with an open palm and a loose grip: let them support you, without letting them become you.

In previous seasons of my life, I was a runner and couldn't imagine my life without running. I was a yogi and couldn't imagine my life without yoga. Last year, after an injury, I didn't run a single step for eleven months. I could barely do an upward-facing dog. My ego hurt and it felt like a knife to my identity. I was a failure, or so I told myself.

One day, as I sat on the beach watching my kids run around, it was Fleur who reminded me: 'This is an opportunity to explore another pillar of who you are.' So, I couldn't run, but I could commit to spending more time in nature. I didn't feel like an athlete, but I could lean into my life as a mama.

In the year between injury and recovery, I wrote and sold my next book; a book that I didn't see coming. Instead of starting work at 7am, I went swimming with my seven-year-old before school every morning. On my phone, I have an album of photos of us grinning into the camera after emerging from the water – 217 smiling, joyful reminders of the year I 'failed' at my habits. It was one of the best years of my life.

This is my advice as you navigate this book: stay open, stay soft and trust wherever it leads you. Perhaps you'll adopt a habit or two, or you'll simply realise that habits can morph and change with you. One thing is for sure: at a time in the future when your 'must-do' habit is taken from you, this book will remind you that there's always another option and another way to come home to yourself.

Introduction

From Routine to Ritual, Simple to Sacred

By Fleur Chambers

A warm mug of coffee in one hand, my mala beads in the other, I toss my favourite blanket over my shoulder and head outside. I tiptoe across the grey stone pavers dotted through the grass in our backyard in Melbourne, so as not to get my woollen socks wet. It's 6am in early autumn. I notice, with delight, the dew that has settled like tiny diamonds on the tallest blades of grass beside me.

I sit on our outdoor couch and settle in. I tend to myself like a bird tends to her nest, paying attention to the smallest of details. Legs crossed. Blanket tucked under both my feet to keep the cool morning air at bay. Whilst I've been meditating for over a decade, I've only been practicing outside before sunrise since the first day of this year, 2024.

Prior to this, there hadn't been anything wrong with my daily meditation practice, nor had I planned on switching things up. But that's the thing about the parts of our lives that become sacred

– they often start simply and spontaneously, untainted by the heavy expectations or pressure that accompany so many aspects of our days.

Perhaps as you've gotten older or your life circumstances have changed, some of your trusted habits have changed too. Has that five-kilometre run transformed into a walk with your friends or pet, where it's more about the journey than the destination? Or maybe your habits have grown in intensity lately as you've found your fitness groove post pregnancy or started writing, gardening or painting now that the kids have left home. And do these shifts allow for less pushing and striving, and greater enjoyment and flow?

I did not wake on the first of January this year and say to myself with unwavering conviction or a heavy hand, *My new year's resolution is to meditate outside every morning this year.* But, somehow, over one hundred days into this rotation around the sun, intuitively, I know I will. Why? Because this simple habit has become a cherished ritual of mine – its golden thread weaves like the morning light into the fabric of my day.

At the end of my meditation practice I make my way inside, bringing with me a sense of freshness and vitality. I grab the kids' lunchboxes and smile to myself knowing that, whilst I've done this over a thousand times before, today I shall make my three teenage boys their school lunch as if for the first time. And, whilst I do, I shall hold in my awareness the tender truth that these precious mornings with all my kids at home won't last forever. This is the gift of meditation, to hold it all with a sense of gratitude, lightness and wonder.

When I first came up with the idea for this book – and this collective writing experience – I knew I wanted it to achieve two things: to give my community the opportunity to tap into their stories and build creative confidence, and to end up with a book that inspired anyone who read it to believe in the power of small commitments. Hence, the idea for *Meditate, Write, Celebrate* was born – a program designed to help each person unlock their inner writer, move through creative blocks and uncover the power of storytelling (you can read more about the program on my website).

Over several months, seventeen individuals from all around the world identified and explored their North Star habits – those regular commitments that act as an inner compass, guiding us back to our values and the ways of life that allow us to feel alive. Each writer set out to explore how these habits supported them during the inevitable highs and lows of life. The result is a beautiful, diverse and honest collection of daily habits from writers who range in age from their twenties to their seventies; many of them embracing habits they never saw coming; habits that surprised them and inspired them and reminded them that to feel alive you must remain open.

As a meditation teacher with a diverse international community, I spend a great deal of my time exploring ways to make healthy habits stick – not only meditation but any daily practice that will help the people in my circle to live more fully. I know that the key to cultivating a meditation practice that stands the test of time is to make it personal and enjoyable. Mala beads or no beads. Cross-legged or lying down. Guided or unguided. It's less about following a formal script or 'doing it right' and more about tuning into what feels good for you.

Humans have a complex relationship with habits. We buy books about habit creation and attempt to master the four stages of 'cue, craving, response and reward'. We try and mimic the habits of highly successful people. All the while, secretly resenting habits for their repetitive and chore-like nature. I don't know about you, but I don't need to listen to another podcast about a white male billionaire who gets up at 4am.

Instead, this book offers a refreshing way to identify, explore and deepen the commitments we make to ourselves. With stories from America, Australia, Bangladesh, Japan, Malawi and Vietnam, this book celebrates the power of simple habits that, when practiced mindfully, have the power to ripple into our past, present and future.

These stories also highlight how, in moments of grief and heartache, when we get caught up with the idea of climbing the corporate ladder, or following our passion and advocating for radical change, we often turn our backs on the things we need the most: self-care, slowness, nature, tenderness, connection.

As I've read these stories alongside my editor, we've both laughed, cried, grinned from ear to ear, and sent messages back and forth to each other: *Oh wow, that chapter is going to stay with me forever.* We've been in awe of the scenes that we've been invited to share through these stories: a puppy abandoned in the forest, a pod of dolphins connecting someone with a loved one, trees with a sense of humour, skies that speak and rivers that heal.

These are stories of how the small commitments we make to ourselves ripple out into different aspects of our lives in remarkable ways: softening our childhood scars, helping us to reconcile our past, forgive others and ourselves, and strengthening our relationships with our own children.

I know every person who reads this book will receive the message they are meant to hear: a gentle nudge to slow down and spend more time in nature; a reminder that we are never too old to try something new; an invitation to take social and environmental action or to reconnect with our own sense of hope and belonging.

For me, the daily habit of meditation has been transformative on a variety of levels – many of them unexpected. How awesome it is to reflect upon the truth that meditating on my children's floor as they fell to sleep over a decade ago has led to teaching meditation to people across the globe, writing two bestselling books and supporting others around the world to celebrate and make meaning of their lives through meditation and storytelling. But that's the power of ordinary habits –

they often create extraordinary impact.

The truth is, your habits not only benefit you, but also the people around you. Nothing happens separately in this close-knit universe. If I meditate, it means I am more likely to enjoy a moment of connection, maybe even a laugh, with the person who serves me at the supermarket. If your doctor has been for a cold-water swim that morning, they may still be enjoying the side-effects of a dopamine boost when you walk into their clinic: a sharp memory, less brain fog and a heightened curiosity. If you have a good night sleep because you turn off your screen an hour earlier, you won't experience the empathy loss that can go with insomnia or disturbed sleep. Now, maybe, you're more likely to support that charity or offer a helping hand to a co-worker. And that co-worker will be less irritable with their kids when they get home from work. No habit, or its side-effects, exist on an island.

I will let my writers tell you about their personal life-changing habits, but, what I will say is there is something in this book for everyone. I am confident you won't get to the end of these seventeen stories without thinking about your day (and your life) through a new lens, excited and hopeful to make the changes you've been craving in an enjoyable and achievable way. Or maybe you'll see with fresh eyes and greater appreciation your current habits, and the gentle way they anchor you to your values and what really matters.

We don't need state-of-the-art hiking boots to enjoy the mountains or the latest tracker for our daily walk to 'count'. We can enjoy writing without an expensive leather-bound journal or cooking in the absence of the latest appliance. Engaging mindfully in our habits is more important than looking or feeling the part.

Beginning my day outside in meditation reminds me that life is always changing and that I can feel safe amidst the movement. This morning ritual allows me to soften that sense of bracing, controlling, wanting and planning. It also helps me to recognise the impermanent nature of my life. When challenges come my way – like sick kids, periods of anxiety or relationship upheaval – I can remind myself that things change. When moments of joy or happiness greet me, like a belly laugh with my teenage kids or a rewarding interaction at work, they are even more special because of their impermanent nature.

Sitting in the dark before sunrise, I notice that as my breath moves from my warm body and meets the cool morning air, it leaves a trail in front of me. What a miracle to see my breath merge into life. As I gently exhale, I imagine my breath greeting the trees in my neighbourhood, weaving its way through their branches. Every aspect of these trees receiving my carbon dioxide like a gift. As I inhale, I thank these same trees for providing me with fresh oxygen and life force.

I remember that my breath tells a story. This breath of the early hours contains the memory of my dreams, the narrative of my week, the hopes for my day. This breath connects me to my parents and my grandparents. I can even imagine this flow of breath travelling through time and space, all the way back to the first creatures who came out of the water over three hundred million years ago, fins to limbs, water to land.

I end my meditation and my time outside like I always do, by repeating silently in my mind:

Today is a new day that I have never seen before. And for this, I am deeply grateful. May I move through this day with a sense of freshness, wonder and trust.

May this collection of stories help you reflect on your own experiences, identify your North Star habits and celebrate the impact they have had on your life. Together, let's remember the power of returning to the things that make us feel good. From routine to ritual, simple to sacred, these habits remind us that everything is connected, and we are indeed part of the great mystery of life.

Chapter One

Feeling all My Feelings

When Brenda Lee Nelson faced the death of her father, she discovered a daily habit that helped her deep-dive into her emotional world and pull at the threads of the 'cultural cloak' she'd been wearing since childhood.

Even though we had talked the night before, I knew he was gone. My dad was 'snow birding' halfway across the country, one of the many people who migrates to warmer parts of America in the winter. At the time, he had been receiving treatment for cancer for less than five months. Every Monday, I would log on and check his labs online, after his weekly check-in with his care team. I always felt a sense of hope whenever I logged on. Up until now, the labs had been a rollercoaster of good weeks, bad weeks and everything in-between.

This time when I pulled up his medical chart, the labs were blank. On the lines that usually held his white blood count, red blood count and blood pressure, there were empty spaces. No numbers at all.

I felt a definite sensation in my body, like someone had grabbed onto my insides and twisted them, followed by a sinking feeling. I tried to call Dad. No answer. He always answered my calls. My entire bodily system went into a panic. I called the clinic; he hadn't shown up for his labs. The world around me started to spin. I called my sister. She tried to soothe me, telling me that he was probably fine. She would call the local police and ask them to do a 'wellness check' on Dad. I agreed … but I knew. I knew he wasn't fine.

On this sunny, sorrowful day in May of 2016, I learned the news that my father had died – the first parent that I would grieve. But it was also the beginning of my awakening to my own body and to a life fully lived.

Research shows the death of a parent is a significant 'life course transition' for people. No matter how old you are when a parent dies, it can spark a rush of change that impacts how we view our careers, our health, our relationships and ourselves. Many people feel this, and it was certainly true for me.

I had long been a daddy's girl. My parents divorced when I was thirteen. My older sister left with my mother, while my younger brother and I continued to live with Dad in our childhood home. I hold vivid memories of my dad playing games with us outside and teaching me to do a front handspring. It was my dad who taught me how to flip an egg without a spatula and how to safely use a chopping knife. Another of my happiest memories is even earlier – when the snow would fall, I would bundle up and ride at my dad's feet on the bobcat while he plowed the driveway.

My dad was a very hard worker and I'd adopted his ethic. When he died, I was forty-eight years old, living in a suburb of Minneapolis while juggling a corporate job and on the tail end of raising three children of my own. Up until this day, my life had been packed with things to do and people to see. There had been no down time nor extra time for things that I couldn't post a picture of on social media or check a box off for completing in my planner.

There had also been no time to feel or process emotions. Before the death of my dad, I would have proudly told you that I'm a 'glass half-full person'. In truth, I had just become very good at sweeping anything that felt 'bad' or 'negative' under the rug. I wore positivity like a badge of honour. It was normal for me to put on a happy face and to just keep going no matter what. But, upon confirmation of my beloved dad's death, that mode of operating was no longer available to me – and this shook my identity to its core.

In the early days, and weeks, after my dad's death I remember doing a lot of sitting, thinking, dwelling. What I wanted more than anything in that moment was to have my dad back; to somehow rewind the clock. I went over the conversation that my dad and I had the night prior during our daily phone call. *Had I missed something?* When I had asked how he was, he said he felt 'weak' – but he always felt weak after his chemotherapy treatments. Should I have known this time was different?

As I reflected, the pain I felt in my own body was both excruciating and, oddly, welcomed. It made his death, and my grief, feel more real to have a tangible, physical sensation to attach my swirling thoughts to, like an anchor.

In those early days, I made a promise to myself: to honour the love for my dad by feeling every single emotion that arose from his passing *in real time*. I would no longer stuff any of them down and act like everything was okay if it wasn't. I didn't have a choice, if I'm honest. My grief was so immense that all I could do was surrender to it. To sit in stillness and stare out the window. To laugh and cry with my siblings as we shared our memories of Dad with each other. Some memories we agreed on and others our individual recollections were very different. It did not matter. What mattered was our unity and connection.

And then, the natural trajectory of mourning began to take place. After just a few weeks, the world expected my life to go back to normal. My siblings stopped coming to sit with me (I don't blame them; they had their own lives to lead and their own way of processing). My boss was very compassionate and understanding. He told me to take as much time as I needed. I knew I needed years though, so I returned to work and began to feel what it is like to work AND grieve.

My husband was supportive and yet I knew that he couldn't fully understand the depth of my sorrow as he had not yet lost a parent of his own. Still, he lovingly allowed me the time and space I needed, but I knew it was time for me to return to my domestic contributions as well.

I also knew that I needed extra support, so I began searching for a 'grief group' to help me navigate through my grief journey, but every group I found was tied to a religion. Handing my grief over to God did not work for me. I wanted to fully feel and process the grief myself, not delegate it to anyone, including a higher power.

When I was unable to find the support I was searching for, I created my own process for understanding my grief. Every morning, I wrote in a journal that I dedicated to myself and my dad. I wrote letters to him sharing my sorrow, my regrets, my fond memories, my anger, my guilt and my struggles. I shared the dreams that I was having in which my dad showed up. I wrote poetry and shared it with him. I used it to express all my emotions as they came up. It became one of our special places to connect across the planes. It still is.

Secondly, I began reading books on grief – a lot of them. One of the books I loved was *The Top Five Regrets of the Dying* by Bronnie Ware, a palliative carer. In her book, she shares the number-one regret she hears from patients at the end of their lives: 'I wish I'd had the courage to live a life true to myself, not the life others expected of me.' When I read those words, my whole body tingled. I knew, immediately, it was

When I was unable to find the support I was searching for, I created my own process for understanding my grief. Every morning, I wrote in a journal that I dedicated to myself and my dad. I wrote letters to him sharing my sorrow, my regrets, my fond memories, my anger, my guilt and my struggles.

a sign to pay attention.

As I've shared, I loved my dad deeply, but it was also time to acknowledge the limiting beliefs that he had bestowed on me. My dad worked really hard. He was also playful, tough at times and loving at others. Like the rest of us, he had issues. Some of these were passed down to me and woven into my 'cultural cloak' – a term that I learned later, which means 'to conceal or hide something due to cultural conditioning'.

For me, my cultural cloak conditioned me to cover my so-called negative feelings – at all costs. From my childhood, being strong and hiding my true feelings had become a protection mechanism that I learned from Dad. I can still hear him saying things like, 'be strong' and 'crying is for babies' and 'big girls don't cry'. In my body, I can feel this as, perhaps, my earliest learned belief that led me to hide many of my emotions.

This is not meant in any way to put my dad down. I know from being a parent myself that we only ever do the best that we can in the moment with what we have and what we know. In a way, I am grateful. It is consoling to me to realise that it was *because* of my dad's death that I began to pull the thread of my identity and unravel it all. The thought that my dad played a part in both the creation of my cultural cloak in childhood, and that he was also the catalyst for my beginning to dissolve it in adulthood, feels like a warm glow in my heart.

Over time, it allowed me to explore my feelings towards my grief and myself. Instead of asking, over and over again, *Who am I without you?* the question simply became, *Who am I?* And the answer changed my entire life.

It began with exploring my conditioning around money – the belief that I had to work my fingers to the bone to be worthy of financial stability. I was brought up to believe that I needed to work long tireless hours. To go to work even when sick. I found that this simply was not true. My work and personal life came into balance after letting that belief go.

I also realised that the way I worked was not honouring my body, mind or spirit – sitting at a desk for long hours and working in an environment that was not aligned with my values. At work, I began to take regular walks, going home for lunch and exploring what I truly wanted in a job. I started checking in with my body and the clues it was trying to show me. *Is this expanding or restricting?* For the first time in years, it felt like the universe was working magically *with* me.

All this coincided with the beginnings of the pandemic when the way we worked changed almost overnight. Before my dad's death, when working hard was my identity, I think I would have struggled with working from home. Now, I was able to accept and understand that, when one door closes, another door opens. So, when I was made redundant in 2022, and given an adequate severance package, I decided to embrace the freedom and choices it offered me.

Today, one of my vocations is my work as a certified professional coach. Amongst other things, I support people who seek to find out who they truly are without their cultural cloak. I also like to say that I *work in service of the trees* as the foundation and advancement administrator at the University of Minnesota Arboretum. A perfect organisation for me holding a position that fully aligns with my values. I am doing work that truly feels meaningful – but I am also not attached to it. My body tells me that right now at this time, I am in the right place with the right people, but I am aware that could change tomorrow. If it does, I will notice because I am tuned into my body.

These days, my life moves slower, I don't care about posts on social media or long lists of checkmarks in my planner. I don't schedule things back-to-back with no time in-between to reflect. What matters to me is being true to what my heart desires, no matter what I have been conditioned to believe is 'good', 'bad', 'right', 'wrong', 'acceptable' or 'not acceptable'.

Through this process, I have decided that my ultimate role here on earth is to have a deep and rich human experience that aligns with my own values. To me, this includes feeling all my feelings, knowing that there are no such thing as good or bad emotions. I plan to keep pulling on the thread of my cultural cloak so that I can let all that is not truly me fall away.

The more I pull the thread, the freer I feel. Now I think of my life and my true self as a blank slate – an idea that feels delicious to me. The possibilities are endless, and I can question any thought that doesn't feel good or true in my body. What a shame it would have been to have lived out my life without feeling the full range of emotions.

Some people have an awakening that happens overnight. My experience is still in progress. This was, and continues to be, a tremendous amount of inner work for me that will probably be ongoing for the rest of my life. It means staying vigilant in re-examining every embodied belief to see which ones are truly mine versus those which are learned or adopted from my parents, teachers, friends or society. I have discovered that the cultural cloak I inherited from my dad was only a very small part of the whole. It is my responsibility and desire to be fully in control of my own life experience.

Perhaps a part of you has been sparked as you read my story and can imagine how peaceful it would feel to let the beliefs that you carry that don't truly belong or align with your values fall away. Maybe a part of you resonates with wanting to live a life true to yourself and not a life that others expect of you. You don't need to lose a loved one or be on your own death bed to begin.

When my dad first told me that he had cancer, he lovingly said, 'I am going to fight this, but I want you to know that if the chemo doesn't work, I have no regrets. I have left nothing undone.' I wonder if he knew what a gift that was to me. I do believe my dad lived a life

In those early days, I made a promise to myself: to honour the love for my dad by feeling every single emotion that arose from his passing in real time. I would no longer stuff any of them down and act like everything was okay if it wasn't. I didn't have a choice, if I'm honest. My grief was so immense that all I could do was surrender to it.

that was true to himself and not one that anyone else expected of him, and that gives me a sense of peace.

It has been eight years since my dad passed away and I am still uncovering my true self. These days I am more likely to communicate with my dad in my heart than in our journal, although I still recommend journalling as the perfect practice for people who are processing big transitions. Today, my emotions are felt, processed and shared openly. My compassion for myself and for others comes more readily. Because of my years of practice, I can instantly feel in my body when something is true for me and when it isn't. I appreciate the depth and breadth of every single emotion and I strive to always live a life true to myself.

And I still miss my dad every single day.

Chapter Two

My Escape, My Solace, My Reset

Ross Pollard has spent twenty-three years as a paramedic, the last twelve on the helicopter. His time away from work is spent with his wife and kids by the beach. If he is not in the cold ocean, he is taking a daily ice bath.

The text messages are finished, the swim time and location are confirmed: Elwood Beach, Melbourne, 6:10am. It's usually a location closest to my house and I'm always the last to arrive. On this morning, it's still and it's cold. A paramedic, a photographer and a policewoman stand in the sand smiling and talking absolute garbage. The photographer who we both adore is usually the butt of any jokes. I get verbal diarrhoea and blurt out anything that is on my mind as Kendra – the policewoman – and I enter the water.

Some days we stand in the shallows and waste twenty minutes

talking and hesitating before the inevitable. When we are committed, we go straight in and the cold water shoots through our bodies and minds. It's a relief and a shock all at the same time.

Jim likes to sit back on the shore for an extra twenty seconds. We have no idea why – maybe because he is the fastest and is giving us a headstart? We surmise that he is prancing on the beach for show, even though it's the middle of winter and we are the only ones on the beach. But eventually, he joins us.

After twenty metres of swimming, we find our rhythm and meet at the first pole. Jim normally first, then me, then the ever-determined Kendra. She doesn't even stop; she rounds the pole and gives a thumbs-up as she continues as if to tell us she is okay and let's do this.

Did I say rhythm? I meant sandwich or the full 'sanga'! Jim to the left is the first slice of bread, I'm in the middle as the filling and Kendra is the other slice of bread to the right. Commonly, Jim cruises slightly ahead and is my reference point for the pace. I look to my right and there's Kendra – the country girl with the determination of a prize fighter – doing all in her power to keep the pace. Her eyes through the goggles look like a great white shark about to consume a large fish or swimmer.

The water is never the same, however, autumn and winter are the clearest and the coldest. To look underneath the water is like something out of Harry Potter. There are greens, blues, stones, rocks, seaweed, sand, fish in schools and alone. The cold water glides over our bodies like a magic liquid soothing, cleansing and resetting our bodies and minds to their purest form.

As our bodies begin to acclimatise, we are lost in the moment. I love watching my friends on either side of me, with happiness but also an empty mind, as I cannot focus on anything but staying calm in the icy-cold water. If we could scream with delight, we would. We stop at different checkpoints and smile at each other. Who will speak first?

I love watching my friends on either side of me, with happiness but also an empty mind, as I cannot focus on anything but staying calm in the icy-cold water. If we could scream with delight, we would.

Sometimes I just can't wait! We call over the water, 'How good is this?' and, 'I needed that!'

As always, I am overwhelmed with gratitude for the habit that struck me, like a lightning bolt, sixteen years ago: cold water swimming. It was my wife who suggested it as her grandfather was an 'ice berger' (cold water enthusiast) and addicted to the high it gave him.

I've always loved the water. Born and raised in Melbourne, Australia, from an early age I was in swimming lessons, at the pool or at the beach. It has always calmed me but, during my late teens, the pool water started to annoy me. I felt hot and itchy when I got out. Despite the fact I live in Australia, the ocean water can get as low as nine degrees Celsius in the depths of winter, which might not sound cold to an ice berger from England, but it was enough to keep my teenage self out of the water for three seasons of the year.

As an adult, when I rediscovered ocean swimming, something had shifted. I didn't abandon the ocean as the weather got cooler – in fact, I embraced it. No wetsuit, just a wetsuit hat. It became a type of meditation for me. In the water, any thought or distraction would throw me off, so I was required to stay in the moment. It worked and I had complete mindfulness. I finished my swims with a steam and a hot shower. The contrast was amazing, and I always left for home in an amazing mood. Whenever I felt shit or something was getting me down, my wife would send me off for a swim. It was just brilliant – a complete cleansing of the brain and body. I would return home a new person – calm, happy, unaffected and less reactive.

The therapy of the ocean and the cold water is a well-researched and proven phenomenon. The late marine biologist and great waterman, Wallace Nichols, calls it 'blue mind'. He says, 'When you see water, when you hear it, it triggers a response in your brain that you're in the right place. The blue mind is neutral, neither overly positive nor overly negative. It's Zen, it's the middle way, it's mindfulness. It's joyful. It's chill.'

As a paramedic, my work has always been stressful – we see trauma and tragedy daily – but I was good at my job and had been totally committed for over a decade. Then came 2019. I had been bullied at work and I finally spoke up. My concerns were not taken seriously and to my complete shock, I was stood down from my job for an 'unspecified time'.

When your job gives you a huge part of your identity and it's suddenly taken away, it's easy to feel untethered, angry and lost. My mind spun and I went into full depression and panic. So, every day while suspended from my role, I went home to the cold water – and for that hour nothing was wrong. The water also helped me process the strong emotions running through my body.

Maybe you've experienced the feeling of losing your job overnight, or the loss of any part of your core identity. For two decades my weeks revolved around sitting in an ambulance and, later, in an emergency helicopter with one focus: helping people. When you've had that kind of purpose for most of your life, it's a strange and surreal feeling to have it taken away, even if it's just been put on pause. This is where the benefits of cold water swimming went far beyond a form of exercise or a way to get an endorphin boost – it taught me to embrace and accept all kinds of hardship. Every time I was challenged by the cold water, I was conditioning my mind and body to overcome the challenges I was facing at work.

I had a light-bulb moment with a fellow cold water swimmer in his shop, *The Grumpy Swimmer*. He said, 'Don't speed up to warm up. Accept that it is cold and go from there. Start off slowly and enjoy it. It's just cold water.' It was so true, and it took me to another place again – an acceptance of a new zone for my body, mind and outlook on life. A place of resilience, numbness, invigoration and pure joy! It was better than any drug, possession or amount of money.

In the end, I was off work for seven months. When I went back, it didn't feel the same. You can't have false allegations made against you and then go back to work as if nothing has taken place. This is where I fell back on my lessons from cold water swimming again. You are more than your job. Embrace change. Everything is going to be okay. The water is never the same. What you see is never the same, and you must learn to love that.

When COVID-19 hit our city in March 2020, my favourite place to swim – a fenced-in ocean pool – was closed as it was classed as a 'gym'. Until this point, I always swam on my own as it suited me. I had a paranoia about sharks, but I felt safe in that ocean pool. I knew, however, that I couldn't give up on my hobby, so I bit the bullet and hit the wide, open ocean right across from my home – and my joy took me to the next level again. This is also how I became part of an ocean swimming community.

During lockdown, our local beach became busy. I loved all the people I met and swam with. A new joy opened for me, and I would stop and enjoy the views and sensations with all the other people as we swam in the cold water. We called ourselves 'Team Shrinkage', named after the *Seinfeld* episode where George Costanza notices what happens to the male appendage after swimming in cold water.

Then came the dolphins... right here near Melbourne! Unbeknownst to me, Kendra had lost her brother to cancer as a child and it was his anniversary. Before our morning swim, she had sat in the car crying – Jim and I knew nothing of this. We all swam and enjoyed the peace and stillness of this beautiful winter morning. The water was crystal clear, there was no breeze and it looked like glass on the surface.

As we swam to the shallows, I heard a scream, not in fright, but pure excitement and joy. Jim and I turned to see a pod of dolphins swimming past us with one swimming behind Kendra and gaining on her as if to say hi. She told us afterwards about her little brother's anniversary. We were in their world, and they came and checked on Kendra. They knew she needed that moment. I get goosebumps just thinking about it.

If you don't live near an ocean, the thought of seeing fins rising about the surface might seem terrifying, but it's not. The most amazing part is, when dolphins do appear, no-one gets frightened. They swim under us on their backs and look up at us smiling. If we stop and scream and shout with joy, they leap out of the water around us and then swim off again. I've never felt so insignificant and so happy at the same time.

I remember one day, when we were a fair way off the beach, a pod appeared jumping, twisting and turning and herding fish in for a feast. My friend Kerry shrieked and swam to me, and said, 'What do I do, what do I do?' I replied, 'You do nothing and enjoy, and they will decide when to leave.' At that moment, one twisted in the air next to her, swam around her and then peacefully swam away. Kerry floated back to the beach on cloud nine.

These days, our ocean swimming group is smaller. After the COVID-19 restrictions eased, people went back to the gym or their respective ocean pools, splintering into smaller groups. This is how Kendra, Jim and I came to swim together. Each of us has different backgrounds and experiences but with the same joy and passion for ocean swimming, particularly in the cold.

We often stop and look to the city in wonder at where we are in that moment. As the swim finishes, we congratulate and thank each other. We then disappear back into our respective lives contented and at peace. We all live in the same area yet lead different lives but always come together with that same passion for the cold ocean.

So, what does it do to my mind? It takes me back to freedom and simplicity and insignificance. It makes me focus on one thing which is basic and nothing but pleasurable. Physically, it massages me, throws me around and makes me respect it. It works out my upper body and it soothes and cools my skin. I exit the water reborn and ready for anything.

When I'm in the cold water I am free. I am a child again in the simplest of pleasures. I'm cold, I'm pushing myself and it is silent. I see fish, stingrays, other swimmers and my arms creating movement in the water. Sometimes the rain falls as I swim, sometimes the sun shines upon me.

The cold led me to the Winter Rip – a non-wetsuit swim 3.2km across the entrance to Port Philip Bay, the gateway to Melbourne. We'd done it in summer before and it was pleasant. When we first jumped in for the Winter Rip, it was a balmy twelve degrees. We'd been preparing in nine degrees. It was magical to begin with, losing ourselves in the large rolling swell. Then our safety escort paddler pulled out and we lost sight of the other groups.

To be honest, I wanted to get out right there. I was cold. The waves were large. I felt out of my depth in every way. But I knew I couldn't back down. I would not enjoy the drinks that night if I did, I couldn't pull out. The swim took ninety minutes from start to finish. As we walked – sorry, hobbled – out over the rocks, we were all hypothermic. We had pushed too far. I spent the next two hours in front of the fire in just my Speedos. Now, that was silly, but we were exhilarated.

My passion is now flowing over to my three young children who are seven, nine and ten years old. Just today I hooted, screamed, cheered, laughed, cried and applauded as they caught wave after wave in the cold ocean water. Each time they re-emerged like a newborn baby – the same happiness and pleasure I feel on my face every time I exit a cold water swim.

There is no pressure for them to become cold water enthusiasts, although living where we are, children wear wetsuits in winter and summer. I just want to give them the opportunity to love what I do, or

I bodysurfed in the cold frigid water. Each time my ride finished, I jumped up with satisfaction and quickly raced back out for the next one. Just in case they ran out. I am eight years old again and waving to my mum on the beach after each wave, so I can confirm with someone that what happened was real and so amazing.

at least, experience it and make up their own minds. Having said that, the thrill I get watching them fall in love with the ocean and its cold water brings goosebumps to my skin and a tear to my eye.

The best part is, there is no age limit on enjoying the ocean. The movie *The Shawshank Redemption* even describes an elderly man's excitement at anticipation of his first experience with the ocean and cold water, when the character Red says, 'I hope the Pacific is as blue as it has been in my dreams, I hope, I hope.'

Author Tim Winton mirrors this delight in the ocean in his book and movie *Breath*, a story about the wildness of youth and learning to live with its passing. His main character says, at the end, as he is reflecting: 'I still paddle out whenever I can. Not to prove anything, just to feel it. That sweet momentum, the turning force, and in those brief rare moments of grace I'm dancing.'

Just last night, as I read this chapter to my wife, I had tears in my eyes of pure happiness. I woke this morning, grabbed my bathers and towel and went to the beach. I didn't swim distance – I bodysurfed in the cold frigid water. Each time my ride finished, I jumped up with satisfaction and quickly raced back out for the next one. Just in case they ran out. I am eight years old again and waving to my mum on the beach after each wave, so I can confirm with someone that what happened was real and so amazing.

Cold water is my source, it's a turbo boost I feel from the ocean. After the swim, I exit and dry myself. I take a shower and dress. I sit somewhere quiet and drink a tea. I'm present but I am all alone in peace, happiness and contentment because the cool ocean has reset me. I'm okay again because I have had my medicine.

Chapter Three

Words From My Grandmother

Born in rural Malawi, as a child, Mercy Kafotokoza decided to become a nurse after the preventable death of her uncle. Today, she is the founder of the non-for-profit Wandikweza, which aims to provide quality, accessible health care to remote Malawians.

When I resigned from my well-paying job as a nurse to start my own organisation in 2016, I used my last pay cheque to register the business and get all the paperwork together. The proposals I sent to potential partners were rejected because the organisation was just starting and had no official 'impact' to report. I struggled to meet the program costs. Worse still, I could see women continuing to die due to pregnancy-related causes even though we had been providing our service to these women for over a year. This fact felt heavy. It made me believe that our services weren't good enough and I wasn't making a difference.

For months I lay in bed at night, berating myself for resigning from a secure job and worrying about how I would pay the bills and staff. I went from being an independent, financially stable woman to relying completely on my husband's income. Within four months of quitting my job as a nurse, I spiralled into fear, confusion and despair. It's hard to admit, but during this difficult time in my life, I also experienced severe depression and suicidal ideations.

Perhaps I would have continued down this dark path and given up on my dreams of running a not-for-profit, except for a visit with my grandmother. When I shared with her how I felt, and the emotional spiral I was caught in, she reminded me of a habit that everyone in our remote village did daily, out of necessity – collecting water from the river.

In my village in Malawai, it is still a daily tradition for women and their daughters to wake up early, when the rooster crows, to fetch water from our local river. I did it from when I was six years old. Every morning, the village women's leader would beat the drum for the women and girls to meet at the village square. We would walk as a team in single file to Namisu river. Almost 3km away from our small grass-thatched roof hut, the river was infested with crocodiles, but it was the only source of water in our village for drinking and domestic use. When going to Namisu river, the girls went at the front so if needed, the women could save them from danger. Attacks from hyenas were common but we continued putting our lives at risk because we had no alternative. As the youngest amongst the girls, I was always in front leading the way with a light that could only ever last a few minutes because it was made from dry grass that burnt as fast as paraffin.

The dusty path leading down to Namisu river was steep and slippery, and we would undertake it no matter the weather. During the rainy season, the river would become fierce, rising in volume and speed, but nothing could stop us from fetching water.

To carry the water back to our village, we balanced heavy clay jars on our heads. The female leader would always tell us, 'You can balance any weight of clay water jar as long as you take a deep breath and concentrate on reaching home.' During these daily morning trips to the river, the women made connections and shared ideas with women from other villages. They formed strong bonds and strengthened the spirit of togetherness.

When coming back to the village, we would sing to alert the men and the boys that we were safely back from the river and that we had conquered the heavy clay jar weights. Then, we would go to the forest to fetch firewood for cooking because domestic tasks were entirely a responsibility held by the women and girls.

This is the habit that my grandmother reminded me about when I visited her and confessed that I was thinking of giving up on my not-for-profit. 'Grandmother, I give up,' I remember saying to her. 'There is too much pressure on me. I don't think I can do it.' My grandmother delivered a dose of tough love. She responded, 'I never taught you that way, giving up is not part of the equation. Wake up early in the morning and fetch water at the river; keep your mind clear and give it space to breathe along the way.' She was reminding me of my strength, my inner commitment and my loyalty to the people I wanted to help; my 'village', which was now everyone who could benefit from accessible health care.

She also reminded me of a promise I'd made to her thirty-five years earlier on the heartbreaking day that inspired me to become a nurse in the first place.

On that morning over three decades ago, I was woken up before the rooster crowed. I was nine years old. I remember lying in my bed when I felt a tap on my shoulder and my ragged blanket was pulled away from my tiny body. I thought it was time to go to the river, but this Monday morning it was different. It was my grandmother, saying urgently, 'Mercy, wake up, it's around 3am, we must go to the hospital

To carry the water back to our village, we balanced heavy clay jars on our heads. The female leader would always tell us, 'You can balance any weight of clay water jar as long as you take a deep breath and concentrate on reaching home.'

with your uncle. He did not sleep last night.' A week earlier, my uncle had begun experiencing a toothache. My grandmother had taken him to a traditional healer within our village, who used a spanner to extract the tooth without anaesthesia, but now it was infected.

At the time, the village healer, Che Wisiki, was very trusted within our community. People turned to her for all sorts of help. She was even attending to pregnant women and conducting deliveries inside her small hut. Women, from our village and other villages, would come with chickens as payment for her services. Some families would ask her to name their babies because they believed that she could talk to spirits to give fortunate names to their children. She even had rooms in her hut where she admitted some serious cases. The community believed that she had special powers to invoke healing spirits.

My grandmother told me that as my uncle wasn't getting any better, she had lost faith in Che Wisiki and her healing methods. Instead, she had sold our two chickens to pay to see a doctor. We had to leave our hut in the middle of the night to avoid people seeing us. At the time, it was taboo to seek medical care without the approval of the village chief, but my grandmother was both determined to get the best help for my uncle and brave enough to go against tradition.

I only realised when I was older that we walked 56km that day. I led the way, just as I did when we went to the river, carrying a light. My uncle had been placed in an oxcart to carry him. I could see him crying and rolling with pain in the cart. My little bare feet walked as fast as they could carry me to reach the hospital. I remember feeling helpless and afraid.

We walked in a single file between tall green grass. It was March, the rainy season. We took some banana leaves with us to act as umbrellas in case it rained. It was also very hot. My grandmother had taught me how to use the sun to determine what time it was. Noticing the shape and length of my shadow, I knew it was noon and we had been walking eight hours.

As the day went on, my little feet struggled to carry me. I remember my grandmother gave me some roasted nuts and water to revive my body and my spirit. She begged the man directing the oxcart to let me sit inside the cart. As the sky became red and the sun moved towards the horizon, we reached the hospital. My uncle was admitted – and died two days later. The nurses told my grandmother that my uncle's condition had been treatable, but he came to the hospital too late. I will never forget my grandmother crying and saying, 'If only I knew, if only I had come with my son earlier, my son would still be alive.'

On that sad and difficult day, my grandmother and I each made a promise to one another. I promised that when I grew up, I would become a nurse and work to avoid preventable deaths in our family and community. My grandmother promised to be by my side always; to give me the necessary support to achieve my goals, and to always cheer me on.

As a child growing up in Chikhala village, 120km outside the urban centre of Malawi's Blantyre district, my grandmother knew my only ticket to nursing – and an escape from the vicious cycle of rural poverty – was education. Two months after the burial of my uncle, my grandmother left the village for the city with me, and she began working as a maid. I would never have been able to fulfil my dream of becoming a nurse if it wasn't for her and her dedication. In 2007 I received my nursing qualifications and enjoyed a successful career as a nurse for nine years.

To you, my experience of growing up in south-eastern Africa may seem very different from your childhood and daily experiences, but there are relatable threads. We have all felt helpless, overwhelmed and anxious at different times in our lives. Many of us have embarked on a long journey to pursue a passion or fulfil a purpose and, halfway there, felt like our legs could not carry us anymore. Maybe you didn't have a grandmother or a village to remind you of your strength, but was there someone else in your life who cheered you on and told you to keep going?

Despite the difficulties I was going through in the first year of growing my organisation, after my grandmother reminded me of my promise and also my childhood ritual of going to the river, something shifted in me. The following Sunday morning I woke up at 4am and in my own way, revived the ritual from my childhood. But, instead of walking to the Namisu river, I found a nice comfortable place in my living room where I knew I would not be disturbed. I said to myself, *I am ready to rise again and create a story of my success.* I lay on my back, gently closed my eyes and began to breathe slowly. I tried my best to relax my body.

When my body softened a little, I created an image in my mind of me walking the path to the Namisu river. I heard the voice of the women's leader reminding us to take a deep breath, and that we could carry any weight that comes our way if we concentrate. As I lay on the floor of my living room, I realised that I could take this advice from my past and use it in my own life. The despair and overwhelm I had been experiencing began to lift. It was replaced with a feeling of excitement and possibility. Ideas began to flow. And then it came to me – the image of nurses riding on motorbikes providing care to women in their homes.

Over the next few weeks, I continued to rise at 4am, lie on my floor and connect with this visualisation of the nurses on motorbikes reaching women in remote locations. Each morning, the image became clearer, and I felt more inspired to make it happen. I realised that, when I lay on the floor to breathe, relax and visualise, I was meditating. In this state, everything felt possible and within my reach.

From then on, every morning, I would take the time to sit and revisit the river in my mind. With each day, I became more confident,

When my body softened a little, I created an image in my mind of me walking the path to the Namisu river. As I lay on the floor of my living room, I realised that I could take this advice from my past and use it in my own life. The despair and overwhelm I had been experiencing began to lift. It was replaced with a feeling of excitement and possibility.

inspired and ready for any situation. I started to see new ways of expanding my business. I began to understand that the challenges I was facing were an opportunity for me to think creatively and to do my best. Within a year, I had turned that visualisation into a reality by planning and implementing the Nurses on Bikes program to ensure that no pregnant woman or child under five is more than thirty minutes away from emergency care. For the first time in a long time, I was working creatively, efficiently and with a sense of lightness and joy.

As I write this, we have not had a maternal death in our catchment area since 2023, which is simply a miracle. We have fourteen Nurses on Bikes who have supported over 56,000 women and children over the last year. I am more aware of my skills and talents. I have found partnerships that allow Wandikweza to grow. I am energised and the ideas keep on coming. In fact, we're in the process of constructing a neonatal unit to further enhance survival rates for newborn babies.

Instead of rising at 4am and beginning my day by looking outwards as I walk to the river, now I turn inwards. This habit has made me realise that the answers to most of the challenges I face in life are within me. My grandmother lived long enough to see the fruits of the promise I made to her. Two days before she peacefully died, at ninety-seven years old, in February 2024, she reminded me to never give up, to stay connected to the river and to my inner world through meditation.

To find out more about Wandikweza and Mercy's creative and courageous approach to eliminating preventable maternal and newborn deaths, visit: *wandikweza.org*.

Chapter Four

Trail Adventures of a Dog and a Hippie

As a semiretired psychotherapist and crisis responder with a difficult childhood, Ed Jones found forgiveness by walking forest trails – but first he had to learn to embrace the journey and not focus on the final destination.

I have enjoyed hiking as long as I can remember. Thinking back, I realise that most of my life I hiked with one intention, to finish, to complete the task. I did the same when I was a long-distance runner and a long-distance cyclist. It wasn't the going, but the getting there that was important. My late wife and I hiked over thirty-five different trails in the Smoky Mountains of North America, proving that we could master them. My focus was usually where my boots met the trail, not all that surrounded me in the forest.

I didn't notice the various personalities of the trees, the smells of the meadows, the wildflowers tucked away off the path, the wildlife sitting in the trees, flying about, crawling around or swimming below.

I overlooked the sun sifting through the overhead canopy of tree limbs and leaves, the moss on the bark of the tree trunk, mushrooms poking from underneath damp leaves. I wish that I had paid more attention. But despite all my shortcomings as a hiker, I always felt refreshed and renewed after I had immersed myself in nature, the magnet that drew me to the woods again and again.

When I started hiking in my twenties, I certainly was new to this sort of outdoor adventure. As a young adult, my frontier was not forests, but a concrete jungle. I'm a city boy. I grew up in a large city in the United States. And as I was navigating my restless life, I found myself navigating trails of a different sort, the ones only found in this city jungle. These trails were paved. They led me on sidewalks, down alleys, late-night bars, hospitals and jail. I even lived and slept on these trails for a time. Cardboard boxes were my Holiday Inn. Having been kicked out of the family home at seventeen, I felt like I didn't belong. I wandered the streets of the city. I was afraid, but savvy. And, at the same time, I felt free. Have you ever had that feeling? Freedom just being another word for nothing left to lose?

I found a large city park where I joined up with a bunch of hippies. We lived and slept in the park that summer. I think this is where I started feeling that the woods were home. I was safe there. The people were good. My life had its challenges, but for the most part, I was at peace.

My life took another turn when I ventured into the city for some food, hoping to steal table scraps from the fast-food joints. I was sitting on a concrete wall when two pretty women walked by. We flirted and they giggled and showed me the tools of their trade. I smiled and told them that I didn't even have enough money to buy myself something to eat. They got it and they laughed and walked away. Suddenly one turned and walked back to me, wrote down her apartment number on a piece of paper, and said, 'If it gets too bad for you out here, stop by.'

I grew up in a large city in the United States. And as I was navigating my restless life, I found myself navigating trails of a different sort, the ones only found in this city jungle. These trails were paved. They led me on sidewalks, down alleys, late-night bars, hospitals and jail. I even lived and slept on these trails for a time.

I wasn't ashamed. I wasn't hurt. I took that piece of paper and put it in my pocket. About a week later, I took her up on the offer. She let me live with her. She had another teenage runaway girl living there as well. We slept wrapped in blankets on the floor. She found me a job and insisted that I go back to school and graduate. I'm not a religious man but if there are angels in the world, I think most of them live in concrete jungles, not in churches. I lived with this woman until my mother asked me to come home. I did, and I graduated from high school. I lost touch with that angel, but I feel her in my heart, even today. She is hope.

When I went to university, I found a huge forest nearby. I always went there between classes. I told my college friends about it and, yes, we drank wine and smoked dope and did all those hippie things amidst the trees. It was good. Ironically, I received two university degrees to be licensed as a psychotherapist. Initially I worked at a state psychiatric hospital. I worked on the adolescent inpatient and outpatient units. I was self-healing as much as helping them. We weren't much different. However, I had a set of keys that let me enter and leave. They did not! Life is just the luck of the draw, I guess.

I met a nurse there and we married. The marriage did not have staying power, but we had two beautiful sons. Later, I fell in love with my barber. We were great. She loved the outdoors. She loved hiking. She introduced me to the natural world in a way that I had never experienced. I was in love with her, with nature, with life. I had my dark past and she had hers. The darkness blew away while we were on the trails and in the forests. Over time, her drinking became problematic to her friends and loved ones, and even after treatment for her addiction she did not feel worthy of their trust and love. She broke. She could not find a way out. During our marriage, the forest had become a beautiful, bonding activity for us. When I lost her, I lost my passion for nature. Sometimes, during challenging times, we can turn our backs on our passions that make us happy, because they remind us of what we are missing.

After my wife died from a broken heart in 2005, I abandoned the forest. I isolated myself. I danced with the devil and drank lots of his liquor. I went back to smoking a pack of cigarettes a day. I was returning to the darkness that I was so familiar with in my younger days. I was functional yet proficient in masking my dysfunction. My outside did not reflect my inside. And then, in 2009, my special baby brother died. He was forty-eight. After he was buried, I went straight home, changed my clothes and went to the forest. I wanted to be far away from people, and I knew the forest would protect me from them. I hiked and hiked, thinking of my late wife and my brother.

I became overwhelmed with emotion. I began kicking the dirt and leaves and grass on the trail. I grabbed fallen twigs and branches and hurled them around. I was angry! I was angry that alcohol and depression took over her soul like an emotional cancer. Angry that she had taken her life. I realised that I had not sat with my grief and that surprised me. I felt I had done everything that I could possibly do to rescue her, to ease her pain. Still, she chose to end it all. After sitting there in the dirt on the trail I forgave her. Sometimes a love story doesn't end the way we had in mind. That was a powerful moment for me. It is said that forgiveness frees us. I am free and grateful for the lessons from the trail that day.

As I continued my hike, I felt a breeze of energy flow through and around me. It was nice. I stopped, sat on an old fallen log, took out my water bottle and drank. It was very humid that day and I was exhausted, physically and emotionally. When my wife and I used to hike, I hated stopping to rest, determined to get to a self-imposed finish line. On that day, as I sat, I took in the beauty and the serenity of the forest. I wondered what the trees may be thinking after witnessing my tantrum on that trail.

Suddenly, from the corner of my eye, I saw a movement at the far end of the log where I sat. It was dark, it was black; it was an animal. I sat still, and slowly a small black puppy crawled from under the log. Then a second one, then a third. These puppies were wary of me. I took my water bottle, cupped my hand and filled it with water. The smallest pup slowly and cautiously approached me and drank from my hand. After the water was gone, I lightly patted his head. He rolled on his back and exposed his tummy, and I rubbed it.

The other two pups wouldn't let me near them. One tried to bite me. Evening was coming so I rose to leave. I waved goodbye and began hiking away. After about fifty feet, I paused and turned, and at the top of the path was the young pup. He was following me. At the time I was fifty-six years old and had never owned a dog, nor intended on having a dog. I scooped him up and carried him home. On that day, once again, I had received an unexpected gift from the forest, from that trail and from that old tree that had fallen and was home to three abandoned puppies.

Max and I seamlessly adjusted to one another. We were a perfect fit, two misfits who had both been homeless. We travelled together, hiked together, went to outdoor music concerts together and camped together. We moved to the North Country about five years later. My significant other owned a house in the forest. She had a cat, Max had me. A city boy and a city dog, a country girl and a country cat living in a forest in the country.

Whenever Max and I would take our walks through the forest, which we did regardless of the weather, we would stop at a very special tree. It was a cedar. Cedars are an integral part of the local ecosystem. They separate carbon from the air, store water, stabilise the soil, provide habitat for local wildlife, shade for lower canopy plants and add nutrients to the soil.

This cedar was a particularly unique tree, it had its own personality.

Its limbs and branches did not grow straight up like most cedar trees. Instead, the branches twisted and curved and stretched out like long arms, seeking sunlight filtered by a canopy of branches and leaves of much taller old growth forest trees overhead. This tree was so resilient, her body, her trunk, her branches and her limbs struggling for life from the sun and rain.

It reminded me of my journey through my own life challenges. Adapting. Changing. Resilient. Finding a way to survive. One of the tree's branches awkwardly stretched across the hiking trail. It was so low that I had to squat to walk under it. This became a game between the tree and me. When I walked under the branch, I would grab the branch and give it a little shake and say hello. If there had been rain earlier, the tree would shake water from the leaves onto my face as I shook it. Snow would drop down the back of my neck. This became our connection whenever we greeted one another. I later began hugging the tree when I passed. If for some reason I forgot and hiked right by, I would get a little down the trail, remember, and feel sad and guilty, so I would turn around, go back and give the tree a hug.

What happened next left me shocked and dismayed, an experience engrained in my heart forever. On this particular day, Max and I headed out for our hike as usual. There was crisp snow from the night before. It was quiet outside. Whenever there is snow in the forest, everything seems quiet. Nature whispers to you. As we hiked, I sensed this uncomfortable energy, a dark, eerie energy. Something was wrong. I instinctively became cautious. In hindsight, I realised that the trees were sending me a message, a warning. I felt a chill, not from the cold weather, though. It was an instinctual chill.

We came upon a grove of trees, young poplars, maybe ten to fifteen feet tall. Several were lying on the ground, still alive, uprooted, one every twenty to thirty feet. They had been pushed over by someone. I could see tracks in the snow from human boots. Someone cruel had

This became a game between the tree and me. When I walked under the branch, I would grab the branch and give it a little shake and say hello. If there had been rain earlier, the tree would shake water from the leaves onto my face as I shook it. Snow would drop down the back of my neck. This became our connection whenever we greeted one another.

ravaged them. Farther down the trail I came upon my friend the cedar tree. Its special branch had been completely torn off her trunk and was lying across the trail. I was heartbroken. I was angry and sad. I was enraged. I lifted her broken branch and placed it beneath her by her trunk. I hugged her and consoled her. My friend had been violated. Her home, the natural landscape, violated. I believed this was my home, too. I could hear the other trees in the forest crying.

Max and I stood there with them for a long time, and it was at this moment that I realised that my connection to trees was very deep and genuine. We are all connected on earth. My visit to this forest, and my visits to land would never be the same. Nature teaches, if we listen. Just as the plants and animals and the sky and the earth depend on one another, so does the environment and us. We are part of nature's sustainability. Nature gives, asking nothing in return from us. After discovering this cruel event, I felt propelled to want to act and give back to nature.

Over the next few weeks, I shared this traumatic experience with friends. I showed them pictures of my tree. Some of them could not relate. They didn't 'get it' and that's okay. Others wanted to heal my grief. One friend suggested that I get a tattoo as a commemoration and that resonated with me. A friend of mine from Germany drew a sketch from the photo of my tree, and I found a tattooist to join the tree and me together, permanently.

I began reading everything that I could about the wisdom of trees. I watched documentaries. My meditation practice even grew to include connecting to nature. Time outside on the trails, and inside reading, watching and meditating was fuelling my desire to give back to nature.

Over the next year I found myself visiting the land more frequently, being deeply present and mindful. I studied the personalities of the many trees I met. I explored new trails and more nature preserves. During one hike I met a fellow hiker, and we shared our experiences about wildflowers and hiking and the environment. I even shared my incident with my favourite tree. She explained to me that she was a land steward of a natural land preservation group, and she invited me to join them. So, I joined the Grand Traverse Regional Land Conservancy. Their mission is simple, 'protecting natural, scenic and farmlands – and advancing stewardship – now and for the future'.

Today, when I am hiking, I am flowing. I hike slowly. I investigate the land and the environment. I pause often and experience its rewards through all my senses. When I'm in the forest, among the trees, I feel like I am home. I feel the forest embrace me. And I reciprocate. We are connected. We know one another, care about one another, respect one another. I am grateful for the lessons I have learned from the trees and the trails. Here I belong.

As for Max, he hiked his last trail on 21 October 2021. On that morning, we went out for our usual hike, I turned toward him and called for him. He walked a few steps, then his rear legs gave out. He lay there, looking up toward me with his sad eyes. I lifted his limp seventy-five-pound body and carried him home. Our visit to his doctor revealed that cancer had taken over his body. With his vet's help, I sat on the floor of the doctor's office holding Max's head in my lap as he took his last breath. After twelve years of friendship and unconditional love we let each other go. Today, Max's ashes lie all around our favourite Cedar tree, and along the paths that we hiked, day in and day out together.

Now, at the age of seventy-two, I spend my days on trails and bushwhacking off-trail with a group of conservationists. We eradicate invasive plants and insects. We collect seeds from the meadows in the fall and plant tens of thousands of seedlings to continue nature's cycle of rebirth and growth. I spend each day grateful for the landscapes that nature gives us, for her beauty, for her shelter and for how she heals us when we listen to her whispers. And I return these gestures of kindness by learning about her, and with this knowledge taking care of her, respecting her and being responsible for her protection. Here is a groovy dog and an old hippie who have learned to belong on the trails we hiked and from the tree we paused to hug.

Are there lessons on the trails or in the forest for you? Hike on!

Chapter Five

Soup, Song and Self-Compassion

Jennifer Robertson is a wife and mother looking for new and exciting ways to express herself in midlife. She was in her forties before she learned the meaning of self-compassion thanks, in part, to a special Sunday ritual.

When I open my eyes, although the house is nearly silent these days, I can tell it is morning. Through my slightly cracked blinds I can see light. It is March in northern California, which means that one day the sky may be pouring down rain and the next it could be seventy-five degrees outside.

My children are grown up now but before my husband, boys and I moved here almost twenty years ago, I had lived most of my life on the central coast of California. The weather doesn't shift much on the coast. My husband had warned me that I likely would hate the weather in northern California. I will admit that I still don't love our summers, where everything is parched, but spring is wet, green and beautiful. It is also short, so I try to make the most of it.

I quietly make my way out of bed, careful not to disturb a snoring husband or our senior pup in her cozy bed at the end of ours. First, I make my way through a yoga practice, a few breathing exercises and drink some water infused with lemon balm I picked the day before. My body moves with ease today. At forty-seven years old, Sundays are slower than they used to be for me.

The garden is still wet from last night's downpour. A fresh, earthy smell fills the air. The fruit trees hang heavy with the weight of the rain; the sun barely over the horizon. My herb garden looks sleepy, still in the shade for now. I take a deep breath. It is a perfect day for spring soup – the scallions are ready. They have survived the winter; strong, tall and, now, fragrant. Soup always feels extra special when I have something from the garden to add to it, and these bright green beauties are the perfect addition to this week's rotation.

I gently dig up the scallions and shake out the soil that clings to the small white roots. I snip some peppermint for my pitcher of water and run my fingers through the lemon verbena, releasing a pleasant scent in the air. I breathe it all in, grateful for these moments alone in the garden.

The birds have just begun to sing. I remove the fallen leaves and pine needles from their bath and check their feeder for seed. I have a special relationship with birds. We take care of one another and they always remind me of my great-aunt who had come to live with us in our family compound when I was a child, after my great-uncle had passed away. Aunt Mary, too, was a gardener and I learned a lot from watching her slowly make her way through several rows of vegetables in the spring. Aunt Mary was tall with long grey hair she always kept in a tidy bun. She was a quiet lady who mostly kept to herself. While in her garden she always wore sturdy gloves and a big straw hat. Aunt Mary moved more slowly and mindfully than the other women in my life.

One year, when I was a child, there was a large forest fire in the canyon where we lived. A displaced magpie showed up on our property. For weeks, as we watched pieces of ash fall from the sky, this bird lived with us. He loved to sit on Aunt Mary's head while she worked in her garden. I remember looking out our ranch house window to see her pulling weeds with her dog, Sonya, while this bird perched upon her straw hat. The birds in my garden do not typically sit on my head but they do shower me with song every morning, reminding me that there is goodness and peace in this world, even on the hardest days. They also remind me there is often someone watching over us, even if our caretakers are unable to do so themselves.

Back inside, I turn on the music as I gather the rest of the ingredients. I light a candle, marking this time as sacred, before I proceed with my Sunday ritual. It's the time of year when the sun fills our kitchen with light early in the morning. It makes the perfect mood for spring soup-making and dancing. Between chopping, blending and stirring, my voice grows louder and stronger. I think of the birds outdoors, unafraid to sing loudly. This too is part of the soup process.

I do my best singing and dancing while making soup. Somehow, it all blends together. I have found that as my voice strengthens in the kitchen, I am better able to extend my voice elsewhere as well. I am learning to voice my concerns and care in ways I once could not – and it all starts here in this kitchen.

If you were to look through my kitchen window and see a woman making soup, you might think, *What a wholesome, heartwarming scene,* and it is. But it is also more than that. I used to be a person who did not allow myself this time or kindness. I was caring and accommodating to those around me, while being very unkind to myself. My default mode was to push myself beyond my boundaries and criticise myself throughout the day for not doing more or being better.

Anxiety made up much of my childhood and more of my adult life

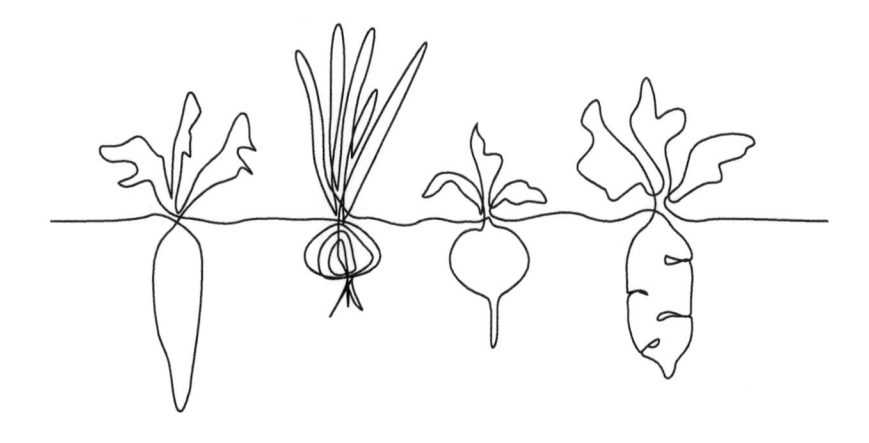

I do my best singing and dancing while making soup. Somehow, it all blends together. I have found that as my voice strengthens in the kitchen, I am better able to extend my voice elsewhere as well.

than I like to admit. Though this anxiety changed shape throughout my life, it was always there, touching nearly every interaction and experience. Like the overcast weather of my younger years, anxiety hung over me, clouding my vision. There was not much flow in my life and there was even less kindness toward myself.

As a homeschooling parent for almost twenty years, I often micromanaged my children's days and activities. Some of that was a natural component of educating my children at home, some of it my own fears and anxiety running the show. As a person who had grown up with family members who were often neglectful, and feeling unloved often, I had committed to being sure my children never felt that way. Like all good things, however; it is easy to go overboard. I can see now, sometimes our best intentions set us up for disappointment in ourselves. Sometimes we are holding on so tight to getting things 'right' we forget to let things flow naturally and we create more friction than flow.

Perhaps there are elements to my story that sound familiar to you. Maybe you are a person who understands how it feels to try so hard to care for everyone around you, you forget to take care of yourself. Maybe you are not a stay-at-home parent like I was but maybe you do feel the pressure to be more and do more, whether it's in your work, your relationship or your role as a caregiver. I think it is impossible to live on this planet without some level of anxiety that sometimes leads us to push ourselves too hard and to the wrong places.

I was forty-two years old when I could no longer deny that my anxiety had trapped me. Though I had seen therapists off and on throughout my life, I never went for more than a couple of sessions at a time. Each time I decided it was too hard and unnecessary. I really did not want to look that deeply at my life and convinced myself that, if I simply focused on the good things in my life (like my children and my husband), I did not need to sit and talk to a professional.

In fact, I did everything I could to not go to therapy. I exercised too much, I focused on my diet and tried to 'stay positive' while inside I was building more and more anger toward myself and my past. Even with years of journalling, yoga and meditation under my belt, I had never learned what self-compassion looked like in action. I had shown grace and understanding to people in my life who had hurt me deeply but I had been unable to do the same for myself.

In 2018, my grandfather was dying and I had not seen or spoken to my mother in over ten years. I did my best to go into the difficult situation with nothing but love, forgiveness and compassion, but I came out of our reunion feeling shattered. The shame, loneliness and blame that I'd carried since I was five years old came flooding back and knocked me completely out of the safe place that I had attempted to create with all of my self-healing practices and self-help books over the years. It turned out that despite my best efforts, some of my deepest wounds had not been mended. I decided it was time to heal my past so I could live more fully in my present.

I remember sitting in my first session with my current therapist – the therapist who patiently guided me into self-compassion and loving boundaries; who lifted the veil on the complexity of my childhood; who forced me to see the scared little girl who would sit, for hours, watching her great-aunt out the window. Early in our time together my therapist explained to me that I had deep compassion for everybody in my life – except myself. She was very firm and direct when she told me what she observed in my behaviours: I believed that other people were deserving and I was not. She was also incredibly kind and supportive, something I lacked from women in my life at the time. She helped me to understand that I was important and worthy of love, care and forgiveness.

It didn't happen overnight, and I am still in therapy five years later, but slowly I began to allow myself time and space to care more deeply for myself and my anxiety. I finally began learning how to tune in

In fact, I did everything I could to not go to therapy. I exercised too much, I focused on my diet and tried to 'stay positive' while inside I was building more and more anger toward myself and my past. Even with years of journalling, yoga and meditation under my belt, I had never learned what self-compassion looked like in action.

to my body to figure out how to best nurture myself. Soup is just one small step in this journey but it has had a big impact. Though I've considered myself a gardener most of my life, especially when my boys were little and still enjoyed getting muddy with me, soup-making didn't really take on significance in my life the way it does now until I began therapy. I like to think my skills in the kitchen have grown alongside my own self-compassion.

Soup-making is not only a sacred practice in my week, it is a great act of self-love allowing myself to enjoy the sights, smells and tastes of my garden. This act connects me to nature, to source. It is also a time to slow down and be with myself. It allows me to feel cared for, nourished by the earth, my own hands and my intentions.

I am someone who has learned that nature, food and movement are medicine. Combining the three feels like magic to my nervous system and sends a powerful message to my brain that I am safe and worthy of this time and self-love. We live in such a hurried and draining world, I believe it is essential to find a rhythm in our days and weeks that allows ourselves to tune in and listen to our own needs, and then actually take steps to fulfil those needs. Soup is a deep spiritual practice for me.

So, what is your version of making soup? It does not have to be an expensive or complicated process – it simply must feel nourishing and authentic to you. I wonder if you too have an activity in your life that wakes up your senses and makes your body come alive. Maybe, for you, it is not in the kitchen or garden. Maybe it is hiking, or paddleboarding or yoga. Perhaps it is a sport or tabletop gaming. It could be making music or art, or caring for animals. Maybe it is volunteering. The point is that you allow yourself the time and space to do it regularly.

When I don't allow myself to be in this flow often, I can feel my anxiety quickly grow. I feel myself getting stuck in my head, in my worries and in my negative self-talk. The more I listen to these negative stories about myself the harder it is to get out of this stuck place. It becomes a vicious cycle. Soup is my reminder to love myself even more during these times and break free from this pattern. For me, self-compassion isn't about ignoring your so-called flaws, it's about understanding that the way we act, especially towards the people we love, is usually a self-protection strategy.

Compassion researcher, Dr Kristen Neff, says: 'The only way to truly have compassion for yourself is to realise that these neurotic ego cycles are not of our own choosing, they are natural and universal. Put simply, we come by our dysfunctions honestly – they are part of our human inheritance.'

When I think back to my own anxiety ten years ago, I can't help but give myself compassion now. I was a person really trying to do the right things, but I was not allowing myself the same care I was giving to others. I see that version of myself and I want to give her a hug and help her feel understood. I wish I could tell that version of me that focusing more on myself, and just a little less on others, would be healing. I am still learning to communicate with my adult children in ways that feel better for us all. It is a work in progress, but something I am better able to navigate now. I can accept my humanness and the fact that I was not the picture-perfect parent I wished to be – and that's okay.

When I sit down to eat a warm, steamy bowl of soup, I inhale all the aromas that come together in perfect balance. My whole body relaxes with each bite. I close my eyes and enjoy. Every time I sit down with a homemade bowl of soup, I feel gratitude for the earth and my ability to grow, just like my garden. This connection grounds me and carries out into the rest of my life. I remember my great-aunt who planted this seed of gardening and mindful living so many years before. I smile as I think of Sonya and Magpie watching over her. I think about how we are all connected, even when we feel lonely and worthless. We all deserve self-compassion and, sometimes, that self-compassion can be found in something as simple as a bowl of soup.

Chapter Six

Stop. Look. Listen.

A passionate ecologist, Dr Melanie Birtchnell hit burnout after the stress of her job took its toll. Rebuilding her life from ground zero, she was angry at the habits that 'failed' her – and then she faced up to a tough truth.

Against a backdrop of one of the worst droughts in Australia, horrific bushfires and the floods that followed, my childhood in the eighties was punctuated by one of the country's most successful road safety campaigns: 'Stop. Look. Listen.' The campaign implored children to cross a road safely by stopping before the curb, looking left and right for traffic, and listening for cars, before crossing the road. This simple slogan worked – as children, we would 'Stop. Look. Listen.' Now my children 'Stop. Look. Listen.' Simple slogans can be so powerful.

Around those same years, a specialist teacher visited my primary school in the outer eastern suburbs of Melbourne, Australia. She came to teach us 'relaxation' – at a time where relaxing in the outer suburbs of Melbourne was done by adults only, around a barbeque. With uproarious laughter, my class scattered our bodies across the classroom floor, amongst eraser shavings and scraps of coloured paper, and attempted to contain our grade four fidgets whilst listening to the teacher's instructions.

What she taught us was essentially a body scan – a kind of 'Stop. Look. Listen.' for our own internal traffic. I struggled to focus my attention, but my body remembered the process and the body scan soon became a regular practice for checking in when my outer world was challenging.

This physical practice complemented the wisdom shared with me by my beautiful Poppa, who taught me how to 'Stop. Look. Listen.' to the traffic of my thoughts and feelings – and to watch that traffic flow past. Like so many boys of his generation, Poppa had left school at fourteen to work. He worked hard and provided for his beloved family. He loved applying his physical strength in body building competitions, yet his intellect was even stronger: Poppa had a great love of classic literature, classical music, philosophy and spirituality. I remember my childhood regularly included sitting in Poppa's cosy study, reading with him – Chaucer, Shakespeare, Confucius, Buddhist teachings and more. When he passed away, I was around thirteen years old and had just finished reading the *Tibetan Book of Living and Dying* – a text he recommended I read and one which helped me process my loss of this special man.

Another vital teacher during my early childhood was an elderly widower who lived at the top of our court. A humble lady with a beautiful garden, she taught me about our ancestral relationships with plants and health and shared with me her knowledge of medicinal and edible plants. Via each plant, she brought to life for me the wonders of nature and again I learnt to 'Stop. Look. Listen.' – this time, to nature. Her love of nature inspired me to study botany and set me on my path as an ecologist.

At the time I was not aware of the important role these teachers played – alongside my parents, siblings, family and friends. However, these three teachers unwittingly changed my life and gifted me mindfulness practices that became my foundation stones for navigating my highly sensitive inner world against the backdrop of the (often highly insensitive) outer world. Without realising it, they had helped transform the 'Stop. Look. Listen.' campaign into a mindfulness practice by which I lived. With my body. With my thoughts and feelings. With nature. I wonder if you can identify your childhood teachers? Who perhaps helped you navigate your internal traffic, taught you to look within or gave you tools by which to safely navigate your life? Or maybe your teachers came later in life? Either way, pause now to consider: who were *your* teachers, who changed the orientation of *your* life? Take a mindful moment to silently express gratitude to them for their teachings – you would not be here, now, without their presence in your life.

Over the decades, these practices held me well, including into motherhood, although anyone with children will know: it is harder to 'Stop. Look. Listen.' to your own immediate needs when you have young children with even greater immediate needs. These practices helped support me to finish my PhD with a beautiful baby in my arms and to deal with the dynamism of my work as a consulting ecologist. Ecology comes from the roots: *oikos* meaning 'our house' and *-ology* meaning 'study', so ecology means 'the study of our house' – this one incredible planet, Earth. Ecology is a diverse job and, although challenging in the face of the looming and devastating extinction and climate crises, it is (perhaps I'm biased) one of the best jobs in the world.

Living your passion and 'reason for being' by working in a purpose-led career is an exquisite feeling. However, for women attempting to combine this purpose-led *need* with the sacred honour of motherhood, it can sometimes bring excruciating friction – friction our society rarely talks about openly. Yes, we are grateful to love our jobs *and* our children. Generations of women before us rarely could choose both.

Who were your teachers, who changed the orientation of your life? Take a mindful moment to silently express gratitude to them for their teachings – you would not be here, now, without their presence in your life.

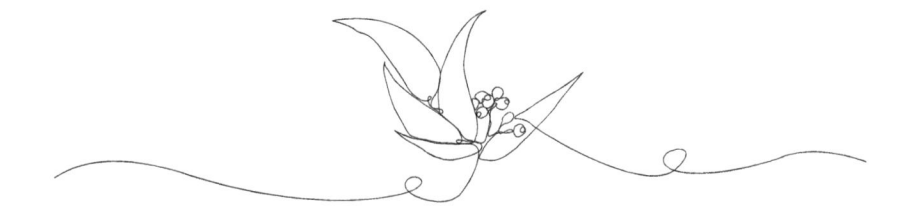

Yet, it is important to acknowledge the significant added stress that comes from juggling your deep love of your vocational work in the world *and* that of your 'other' great loves – a partner and your precious children. Prioritising your energy and time for each can be complex, especially when work and family needs are conflicted.

Ecological consulting conflicted with my family's needs – long days out in 'the field' were not compatible with school hours. To make more time for my family, I swapped ecological consulting for a part-time ecologist role in a corporate environment. Despite working fewer hours, my stress levels increased dramatically. Although my work in this role was some of the most rewarding, impactful and wonderful work I had done, the dense hierarchy of corporate workplaces coupled with the futility of trying to advocate for the environment in such contexts was exhausting, frustrating and demoralising. Often, my tireless efforts undertaking my role to minimise the loss of nature left me feeling helpless. No matter how hard I worked, each approved planning application was contributing to a 'death by a thousand cuts' to nature, to 'our house'. It was so hard to witness.

Two years or so into the role, I learnt I was pregnant with my third child – another environmentalist in the making. When my maternity leave ended, I did not want to go back to my stressful role but felt so limited in terms of where I could continue my meaningful work as an ecologist with hours that could accommodate my family's needs. I felt stuck for the first time in my life. With shame and grief, I resented my career for impacting my family and resented my family for impacting my career. One love impacting another. An impossible stalemate.

I returned to my job. There were incidents that signalled I should leave, yet I stayed. I felt even more stuck. The increasing malignment between my heart, speech and actions was taking a toll on my family life and on my physical and mental health. I was working longer and longer days, often well into the evening. My sleep was erratic and my waking hours were consumed with endless worry. I was running on sheer desperation not to fail, not to break, not to lose my job. I battled on. To battle on with something we know is maligned, we often must ignore our inner voice, or we might have to acknowledge we are compromising on what and who we love. So, rather than acknowledge such painful things, I turned my back on my lifetime of mindfulness practices. It felt impossible to 'Stop. Look. Listen.' – like losing momentum might mean losing everything. I just needed to survive.

I often wonder why, in times of crisis, we let our reliable and trusty practices slide. Despite knowing these 'tried and tested' tools are invaluable and effective to help us navigate challenges, we can find ourselves turning our backs on such supportive habits. Why do we choose not to acknowledge our inner wisdom that could guide us to our 'next most elegant step'? Had I chosen to 'Stop. Look. Listen.' to the messages coming from within, rather than battle on refusing to hear what needed to be heard, I would have been compelled to make some tough – even, seemingly impossible – decisions. I could have chosen a healthy, aligned life. Instead, I ignored my own wisdom and powered on … until I could not power on any longer.

The day my life changed forever started much like any regular day. After a restless night, I had fallen asleep during the early hours of the morning and woken to the early-summer dawn in the mid-2010s. In that beautiful liminal space between sleep and wake, I remember feeling tranquil and soft. But within minutes of transitioning into wakeful awareness, the fears, anxieties and desperation that had been lying dormant behind the scenes during sleep were released in a raging torrent – the cacophony: a distressing and familiar soundtrack to my life at that time.

As I lay there with waves of anxiety consuming me, I felt the most excruciating pain develop in my belly – far worse than any belly pains I experienced during my three home births. The pain was so excruciating it became a raging torrent and, for the first time in my life, I urgently begged my husband to take me to hospital.

Despite myriad tests, the doctors could not find a physical explanation for my symptoms. But as I sat in that hospital bed, I finally heard what needed to be heard: my body was screaming at me to 'Stop. Look. Listen.' I realised in that moment – my life was about to change in every conceivable way.

I was released from hospital with a referral to a psychiatrist, who diagnosed me with burnout and Post-Traumatic Stress Disorder (PTSD). I was distraught by these diagnoses – but not surprised. This isn't just my story. Sadly, in Australia, burnout is estimated to affect at least 61% of workers compared to a global average of 48%. It is thought around 40% of employee resignations are due to burnout, indicating we need to look after ourselves and each other, to help people contribute their unique gifts through their work. How many people who have suffered burnout are ever able to return to their original industry, if they can return to work at all? Devastatingly, how many mothers suffer burnout and cannot readily care for their family *or* continue their purpose-led work? How much does society suffer when someone can no longer contribute their unique passions or live their fullest life?

I found myself there, debilitated – unable to readily care for my family and unable to work. My recovery was long; much longer than I 'expected'. Supportive but helpless, my beautiful family watched on, unable to do the work on me that I had to do for myself. My life and health needed to be rebuilt. Quite literally, even my speech needed to be rebuilt. In the darkest times, I hurled books against walls – adored books on Vedic philosophy and practices that had been the foundation stones of my life for decades. I raged feelings of disgust at how these practices had 'failed' me.

Now, years later, I can see I turned my back on my practices and so *I* failed *myself*. The tools did not fail; I failed to use them.

Yes, we are grateful to love our jobs and our children. Generations of women before us rarely could choose both. Yet, it is important to acknowledge the significant added stress that comes from juggling your deep love of your vocational work in the world and that of your 'other' great loves – a partner and your precious children.

The years between then and now were some of the hardest and richest years I've lived. Yet, I have come to see that difficult time of my life was an enormous gift – the lessons from which helped me rebuild my life from ground zero, from the foundations up. I have consciously curated my life by returning to those mindfulness practices I was taught during my childhood.

It is now eight years since my hospital admission, and my life has resumed its flow of less rigidity, more surrender. Less strategising, more in-the-moment nimble. Less resistance, more softening. I still run around for my family. I work hard, strive for my dreams, and love ferociously. But my life is shored up again with practices I can draw upon, moment to moment. In any moment, I can 'Stop. Look. Listen.' We can all 'Stop. Look. Listen.' – this simple yet powerful practice brings awareness to our actions and choices so we can all live a life where our inner and outer worlds are more aligned, more magical.

For me, 'Stop.' means any way I can press pause and be present: stop doing, talking and thinking. Stop taking on other people's moods and reactions. Stop thinking I have no choice because I at least have a choice of how to respond to every single moment. It means meditation and mindfulness.

To me, 'Look.' means looking inwards and looking outwards. Looking at what my body is communicating to me. Am I moving *away* from fear … or *towards* what I truly love? Seeing what *actually* is happening in this moment, rather than what I *think* is happening. Looking for what there is to celebrate in this moment.

Finally, for me 'Listen' means listening in all the ways: to my heart, my inner voice, my ego and to nature; to what the present moment *actually* is bringing. It involves listening to the silence and to the absence of stories; listening to what is possible as a new way to respond, rather than how I've been conditioned to react.

Every day now, I meditate. I write. I celebrate. Through mindfulness practices and meditation, I have rebuilt my strength and passion for life. I love these practices so much I decided to qualify as a meditation and mindfulness teacher, and now coach my purpose-led colleagues to live and love … mindfully. Pausing to celebrate before rushing into the next task is a 'Stop.' that highlights how much there is to enjoy in life. Writing helps me 'Look.' at my edges and 'Listen.' to them more closely.

With these tools, I have more energy and love for my family. It is joyous to have shared my lessons with them and see my growing children (two teens and a 'tween') experience life mindfully. I have resumed my beloved ecological consulting practice – in a way that is nourishing for my career *and* my family. I am so grateful for the practices I learnt during childhood – and ignored for a while – and for the life I have created with them since, for my family and me. These healthy habits can help us, especially working mothers, navigate the pressures of juggling purpose-led work and a family, so we can continue to contribute in a meaningful way. I love contributing in a meaningful way. After all, ecology is one of the best jobs in the world …

Chapter Seven

Saving Lives

Sal Pollard spent twenty years working as a paramedic in Melbourne. After saving hundreds of lives, she finally realised that the life she really needed to save was her own.

It's funny how some things happen and you remember them as if they were yesterday. The first time I was told I was pregnant and the first time I told my husband that I was wrong were two of these occasions. This is where my story starts and it's also where my story ends – but not for the reasons you might imagine.

Like so many teenagers, I was incredibly shy and unbelievably awkward. Confusion and overwhelm were my constant companions and they dictated my desperate and constant need to fit in amongst my peers, despite every instinct telling me to do otherwise. I wasn't an excited and expectant new mother preparing for the birth of her first child, I was seventeen years old. I was scared and I was all alone.

I'll never forget that sunny afternoon I rode my orange and white bike to see the doctor. It was my most prized possession, probably because I had to save up and buy it myself. I remember riding through the wide leafy streets and feeling the wind in my hair. This was my favourite thing to do because I felt alive and free. Looking back, the irony is almost comical. The moment the doctor told me I was pregnant was also the moment that feeling of freedom left me instantly.

My mind frantically ran through all the options available to me. None of them were appealing. I was still a child myself. How could this be my reality? I desperately wanted to tell someone but who would believe that the condom broke? Or that the morning after pill didn't work. I couldn't see any other option available to me, so I did the unthinkable. I was ashamed, all alone and broken hearted.

I remember waiting in that badly lit room and secretly hoping, in fact praying, that someone would tell me there'd been a big misunderstanding, and all I'd get was a lecture on safe sex. Instead, I saw for the very first time what a heartbeat on an ultrasound looked like, and suddenly the gravity of my reality sunk in. This was the moment my life would never be the same again. I was seventeen years old and unbeknownst to me, I would spend the next twenty years of my life trying to make up for the one I was about to take.

Instantly, I developed an eating disorder. Not because I wanted to lose weight but because food was something I could control. It gave me a sense of power that 'I owned it' rather than 'it owned me'. Of course, this false sense of security was temporary and, like any drug, when the initial hit wore off, I'd be on the hunt for the next quick fix to keep my guilt and shame at bay. Control and self-destructive behaviour became my best friends and I soon traded in my eating disorder for drugs and alcohol. Addiction had crept in like a slow-moving train coming into the station. I knew I'd hit rock bottom when I found myself seriously considering selling my body to buy more drugs. This moment scared me enough to somehow stop using drugs and alcohol as my escape route to dull my pain. Instead, I allowed the dust to settle, but it meant I had to feel my feelings, and when I did, life felt immediately unliveable.

I'd just completed my last year of school and while everyone else was embarking on the rest of their lives, I was on suicide watch in hospital after three failed attempts to end my own life. During that time, I lost every friendship I'd spent the last six years cultivating, I'd put my family through hell, and I was missing out on the best years of my life. I'd never felt so alone.

Looking back now, that time I spent in hospital was all a blur. I couldn't tell you exactly how I survived, suffice to say that, somehow, I escaped the severity of depression long enough to get out of hospital and go travelling. I fell in love with visiting new places and losing myself in different cities. At the core of it, I loved running away from who I was and what I'd done. This would be my pattern for years. I became very good at being a loner and keeping everyone at arm's length, terrified of what they'd think if they discovered the real me.

I don't believe many of us reveal who we really are to the outside world. Do you? Our fear of looking bad outweighs our burning desire to feel that deep connection with another human being. We all have a story to tell, it's inevitable, but we're so influenced by our environment and so conditioned by culture and society that we'd rather hide behind the many layers of guilt and shame, than be vulnerable enough to really be seen. Unless of course, we muster the inner strength to circuit-break this pattern.

Like every other habit and coping mechanism I'd developed, travelling wasn't sustainable. It didn't matter if I was working behind a bar in Belgium or at a corporate desk in London, hiking through the Himalayas or laying in a hammock on my own tropical island. Wherever I went, I took myself with me. My guilt and shame were my constant travel companions – daily reminders of a past that I tried in vain to escape.

I was guilt-ridden but I was smart, and I'd learned to become adaptable. So, at the age of twenty-four, I decided to become a

Looking back now, that time I spent in hospital was all a blur. I couldn't tell you exactly how I survived, suffice to say that, somehow, I escaped the severity of depression long enough to get out of hospital and go travelling. I fell in love with visiting new places and losing myself in different cities. At the core of it, I loved running away from who I was and what I'd done.

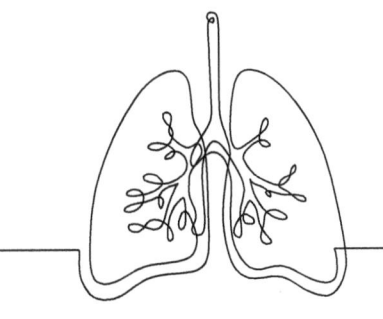

paramedic. My thought process was obvious: a life for a life (or many lives as it turned out). This would be my chance to 'make up' for the one I took as a teenager.

I remember the first time I saved someone's life. He was a teenager who'd taken too much heroin, and someone found him under a tree. He'd stopped breathing and his heart was barely beating. Another minute and he would have been dead. I remember looking at him and thinking this could have been me. We'd both been at that same fork in the road, only he chose to go one way and for some unexplained reason I went the other.

I had hoped that, by saving his life, my feelings of worthlessness would go away. They didn't. Not with the first life I saved. Not with the hundredth. Over time, however, my burden dulled in its intensity, and it became something I just got used to living with. On the outside I pretended I was happy. I met the love of my life who loved me back without judgement. But his love wasn't enough to soothe the sting and nurse the heartbreak I privately felt when we welcomed each of our three children into our lives. Each time I brought a human into the world, I was reminded of my impossible decision and the guilt and shame would come rushing back. I never made peace with myself or what I'd done. I had no idea what true happiness felt like because I'd never allowed it in. In essence, I didn't think I deserved it.

I remember the moment my life was about to turn around. I was walking down the street one winter's morning and was so preoccupied with trying to stay warm I literally bumped into a friend. She talked about this slightly unconventional 'bootcamp for your head', as she called it. Instantly she had my attention. Nothing I'd tried had ever worked and I knew I had nothing to lose. I didn't know it at the time, but that brief conversation would set about a chain of events that would lead me on a path of self-discovery and healing that would set me free.

As it turned out, 'bootcamp for your head' was an unbelievable experience that's very hard to put into words. It gave me the opportunity to process my emotions and release all the guilt and shame I'd been carrying around with me for half my life. It allowed me to stop running away from who I was, and instead, learn how to be with who I had become. It led me to meditation. It was how I learnt the true power that came from really being with myself and feeling everything that lay hidden within.

At first, I hated meditation and I resisted everything about it. It was like trying to train a disobedient dog. My mind had become so addicted to all the reasons and excuses I'd used over the years that it had other plans for us. But something kept telling me this would be my way out, so I persisted.

It's funny what happens when you turn resistance into acceptance. When I finally stopped resisting 'what was' and accepted 'what is' I traded my invisible shackles for freedom and inner peace, and, dare I even say it, some long sought after happiness.

For me, meditation felt like I was coming home. To the outside world I looked calm and peaceful, but on the inside an enthusiasm for life I'd never known before was stirring. I felt like a kid at Christmas. I suddenly had so much to live for. I was beyond excited. I felt like the sun was finally shining on me again like it did all those years ago as I rode my white and orange bike. So, I stuck with my meditation practice.

I learnt more about myself through mediation than I ever had before. There was nowhere to go and nowhere to hide. It was just me. It was as confronting as it was liberating. Over several months, I grew to not only love it but to rely on it. It became so sacred that I began to physically crave it.

In the dark hours of the night, or the early hours of the morning before the rest of the house would stir, I'd find a blanket and warm chair and I'd just be. It was amongst these quiet hours that I learnt to

I learnt more about myself through mediation than I ever had before. There was nowhere to go and nowhere to hide. It was just me. It was as confronting as it was liberating. Over several months, I grew to not only love it but to rely on it.

soften my ego and the many masks I'd spent a lifetime hiding behind. I started to fall in love with the truth of who I really was and all that I'd kept hidden from the world. I felt free.

Like so many things in my life, my 'freedom' also came unexpectedly. For years I had thought that if I achieved or accomplished enough things in my external world, that my internal turmoil would disappear. I couldn't have been more wrong. My freedom came the moment I gave up needing anything in my external world to be different from what it already was. I had made what I'd done as a teenager so 'wrong' that as an adult, I had to make everything 'so right'. I'd learnt the very long and hard way that there is no freedom wanting things to be different to how they actually are.

The first place I let go was with my need to be right. I remember the first time I did this so clearly. It wasn't so much of a conscious decision as it was the next logical thing to do. It was late at night and after putting our children to bed and tucking them in, my husband and I took advantage of what precious time we had left to talk, before exhaustion would quickly summon us to bed ourselves. Amongst our sleep deprivation and lack of any quality time together, it wasn't long before our discussion turned into an argument.

The details, like every argument, don't matter because they were always so insignificant. As usual I made all sorts of excuses and reached for every reason I could find to prove myself right and my husband wrong. Suddenly something came over me and I paused. I stopped yelling and I stopped arguing. I had this insatiable need to give up the one thing I'd been holding onto my whole life – my need to be right.

I looked my husband in the eyes, and I felt everything I'd been holding onto melt away. I told him I was wrong. Neither of us knew what to do. Not another word was spoken. We made love and slept in each other's arms that night. Something in that moment changed within me. I found a strength and an inner peace that I never thought was possible.

By learning to sit with who I am – and love who I've always been – I had turned the guilt and shame that I'd carried with me for nearly thirty years into compassion and self-acceptance. Instead of trying to run away from who I was and what I'd done, meditation allowed me a gentle softness to 'go inward' and to be with myself. This was as powerful as it was surprising, it helped me to finally feel. It was in this feeling place that forgiveness crept in. Forgiveness for trying to erase a past and pretend it didn't exist. Forgiveness for spending the last two decades trying to make up for something I could never change. And most importantly, forgiveness for that seventeen-year-old version of me who was still a child herself, and despite facing an impossible decision, knowing that she chose the best one she could. Because without the wisdom of her past, that awkward teenager wouldn't have grown into the woman I'm so proud to be today.

These days, I spend less time trying to control life and more time enjoying it. Arguing and conflict have been replaced with honesty and authenticity. There is a tenderness I feel towards myself, my past, my husband and our three unimaginable children that allows me to feel so content and happy.

Ironically, the only way to let go was to let go. By giving up my need to be right, I've given up caring about what others think. But more importantly, through forgiveness, I've gained the approval and acceptance of the only person who matters, me.

Chapter Eight

Making My Own Splash

Living with chronic pain, Dr Mandy Mercuri developed an unhealthful way of thinking – constant comparison. Today, she has learnt to live, gratefully, with her condition, thanks to a daily habit that connects her to the wonder of her body.

A circle of luminescent bubbles surrounds me with a sense of calm and playful delight.

Swimming beneath the pink hues of pre-dawn, from the comfort of my own suburban backyard, I float to the gentle rhythm of lapping water and my steady exhales mix with the chorus of birdsong. Laughing kookaburras, chirping and darting cockatiels, magpies singing their good morning song from the branches of a nearby pine tree and the ever-present shrieking cockatoos. I push off from the end of the pool.

Swoosh and thwack, swoosh and thwack.

As my arms travel overhead, reaching forwards, sweeping backwards, I repeat my mantra to keep track of my strokes: 'Arrive. Home. Here.

Now.' You might see a woman in her late forties swimming lengths of her backyard pool in Melbourne, Australia. But this daily ritual goes deeper than that.

Towelling myself off afterwards, the pool is still shimmering, I am energised. This strong, cleansing feeling follows me into the rest of my day.

This is my story about pain, about comparison and about acceptance. It's my bumpy journey to discovering that I had the courage and strength to manage chronic back pain. It's a story about how I forgot my inner strength for a while, was reminded of it and embraced it once again.

Whether or not you've experienced chronic pain, everyone will relate to the disheartening feeling of looking at your own life, looking at someone else's life, and just not measuring up. Comparison is a legitimate evolutionary adaptation of safety. A hangover from those prehistoric days when protection and safety was found within the status quo and solitude meant certain death. These days, whether it is the insidious pressure to meet societal expectations or the unfair burden of discrimination, we all feel it. Comparison lurks, cloaking our authentic nature.

I want to tell you about two major dark times in my pain journey where I have sat in front of a spinal surgeon contemplating a further fusion on my spine. Both of those times were largely a result of falling into the comparison trap. But first we need go back to where things began.

From an early age, as the youngest of five children, my tendency to compare was strong. Will I ever be strong enough, smart enough, pretty enough as my older siblings? I certainly annoyed them all, a constant shadow – watching, copying, desperate to be included and always seeking their approval.

Nothing made me feel more different than when I was diagnosed with scoliosis at eleven years old. My spine was twisted and curved to such a degree that surgery was the only option. Even as a child, I felt like my body had betrayed me.

My awkward teenage years, when I was desperate to fit in, were marred by two major surgeries, months of rehabilitation that included daggy corrective footwear and wearing a solid fiberglass back brace for six months between surgeries. It left me with some gnarly hardware that lights up X-rays like a bionic woman but also embedded unhelpful beliefs that I was beyond different – I was weak, broken, unworthy.

Nothing fires the belly for striving, pushing, people-pleasing and perfection than feeling like you're not good enough. Motivated to prove I was capable and strong, I blasted through my twenties on overdrive, ignoring warning signs of pain, driven towards achievement and showing the world I could do it all.

By my late twenties, the mumbled, grumbled complaints from my body were turning into screams. The back ache felt like my body was made of lead and it was becoming unmanageable. I was functioning on the outside. My scholarship to study mine site rehabilitation in regional New South Wales for my PhD had enabled me to further my research skills and also explore rural living. But when this came to an end, again it was uncertainty that had me stumbling towards an academic career. And that wasn't the only thing I was confused about. I was driven but with a nagging uncertainty about how I could manage in this pain-filled body. I sought quick fixes, multiple treatments and clinicians, a never-ending escalating pain medication cycle … and nothing was working. The pain remained … and intensified.

Desperation started driving my decisions. I wanted to find a way to return to my normal mode of operation – to be back in the game, full steam ahead. I had turned, first, to the medical fraternity to help, but after years of tried and failed clinicians and practices, nothing seemed to work. Looking back, I was searching for a solution outside of myself.

For years I had tried to use various medication to dull the pain but only ended up with increasing doses and more complex side effects. Within a year, I was beginning to struggle with daily activities. Unsure how I would continue to cope, I found myself contemplating further surgery.

After casually assessing my reports, scans and listening to my tear-drenched history, the surgeon sighed heavily, considering. He flicked his eyes to my husband sitting beside me, hand clasping mine. My high school sweetheart, we had recently married, and he had been my rock throughout the journey so far. We were worried and both eager for the surgeon's opinion. What would the future hold for us?

'No children?' the doctor asked. I shook my head, knowing more tears would spill over if I opened my mouth. How could I possibly manage conceiving, birthing and raising children with these pain levels?

If the doctor noticed my heartbreak, he didn't acknowledge it. He continued: 'I would suggest you try to exhaust all possible alternatives first – exercise, get some psychological support, have kids, do your best to stay out of my office for as long as you can …' He had listed them off on his fingers like they were as simple as that. Easy! He looked up at me. 'Try this, then we will talk about surgery.' And with that, I was dismissed.

Never one to step down from a challenge, I did try – I really tried. I continued to seek pain management support and treatments. We even had our first child, my son, after fighting through the later months of the pregnancy exhausted and overwhelmed. How was I going to cope? By the end of that first year after his birth, I was struggling once more. Constant breastfeeding, carrying, hormonal changes and I had spiralled into another dark place. The pain had consumed me once again.

I was referred to a three-week intensive in-hospital pain management course at a major city-based public hospital. There I found hope from an unlikely source – a door in the hospital bathroom. Toilet doors in hospitals open outwards and it took me a week of walking into the door before I remembered and pulled. It was an unexpected reminder that habits can change – even my deeply embedded ways of thinking about pain.

The things I learnt in that course, and the changes I made afterwards, brought about the arrival of a second child (one I had thought I would never be strong enough to deliver). Over the next ten years, our family of four were happy. We all rode the waves of my good days and bad days. I always tried my best and also gratefully accepted their concerned cuddles when I had little to offer.

Then, when I was forty-five years old, a huge pain flare hit. And, this time, it stayed. I had been juggling the demands of a stressful job as the strategic advisor to a family violence regional partnership and the upheavals in family life. I had just completed a half marathon. While it might sound impressive, I suspect my motivations were slightly marred by that comparison grip once again. I had been comparing myself to friends who were runners, so pushed myself into this monumental pursuit mistakenly believing that my own minuscule efforts at exercise like yoga, walking and occasional swims were not 'enough'.

I was struggling with decreasing mood and increasing pain. While I knew all the things that I 'should' be doing, I'd returned to unhelpful habits. On this churning achievement wheel, I began pushing through pain and overdoing it, numbing with alcohol and comfort foods, and distracting myself with incessant busy-ness, resulting in a familiar decline towards exhaustion and overwhelm.

I was also comparing myself again. Wanting to be like other people; wanting to have the important and successful career, whilst maintaining my health and being a Super Mum who volunteered and baked and was constantly happy and always available to her children. That can't be that hard, we can have it all, right?

When pain becomes chronic, neural pathways in the nervous systems can become sensitised. Over time, my brain had unintentionally learned to be in pain! This is referred to as nociplastic pain. In his recent book, *The Way Out*, based on his years of clinical practice, author Alan Gordon suggests that certain personality traits are prone to developing this type of chronic pain – one being the high achiever. All those years of pursuing achievement and upholding my high self-imposed expectations had forced my nervous system into a permanent state of high alert – resulting in this ongoing and debilitating pain.

Chronic pain would be familiar to many. Back pain, in particular, is the leading cause of disability worldwide. Many people fall into the medical roundabout seeking diagnoses, cures and help. Many people are suffering and desperately seek a way to make it disappear. While the evidence points towards needing a holistic self-management approach, the allure of a cure is hard to resist.

Berating myself, I found my way back into a surgeon's office seeking an elusive fix. Different guy, same approach. Examining imaging, absorbing medical history, the proffered tissues. He outlined possible surgery and the likely impacts. Then he surprised me by saying, 'You know, you've done well to manage your pain for the past ten years, why not stay out of here for another ten?'

I paused to let his words wash over me. He was acknowledging the hard work and determination I had shown to avoid surgery thus far, holding up a mirror to my efforts. He reminded me that what I needed was not in his office or on the operating table. All that strength, that wisdom, that courage, it was still there, within me. I had just temporarily forgotten. Turning to my husband and seeking his readily offered reassurance, I took a deep breath. I started with a small step. I offered myself a little kindness and an encouraging thought. Yes, I can handle this!

I reconnected with daily meditation practice, brought in nourishing

I paused to let his words wash over me. He was acknowledging the hard work and determination I had shown to avoid surgery thus far, holding up a mirror to my efforts. He reminded me that what I needed was not in his office or on the operating table. All that strength, that wisdom, that courage, it was still there, within me. I had just temporarily forgotten.

mindful pauses and I sought to connect with a style of movement that would work for me and my body. My kids were older now and, as I looked to the decades ahead, I wanted to ensure I was strong enough to enjoy the coming transitions into retirement, grandchildren and travelling. I had promised myself I was going to be a groovy granny and, for that to happen, I needed to make my health a priority.

Over the years, I was repeatedly told how helpful swimming would be for my pain. As a predominant nose-breather, I often struggled with putting my face in the water ruling out many traditional strokes. So, backstroke was always my favourite. In a public pool though, choked by the claustrophobic humidity, I found it hard to stay in my lane, figuratively and literally. I would compare myself to the 'real' swimmers when I was bumbling along at a snail's pace, staring at the dripping roof, flailing from side to side, whacking lane ropes and the occasional unsuspecting swimmer.

As a child, I delighted in and was fascinated by water. Rain, clouds, waves, wallowing in the bath until the water became cold and my skin wrinkled like a prune, running through the sprinkler on hot summer days. Whenever we went to the beach, I dreamt of being a mermaid then later, a marine biologist studying and conversing with dolphins.

While enthralled by water, I also feared it after having repeatedly chased my older siblings into rockpools and dangerous surf that my little body wasn't strong enough to negotiate. From a young age, I had convinced myself I couldn't swim.

The COVID-19 pandemic and prolonged periods of lockdown made things harder again. Not able to access the supports I had come to depend upon, and with public pools closed, I had to rely even more on my own self-management skills. That year, we moved house and made the family decision to install a backyard pool. Every time I step into the water it is with a sense of heartfelt gratitude, knowing I have been afforded a very privileged position that is not available to everyone.

From the safety of this pool, I began to develop my own style. Slow, steady, focused on being present. I was not training for an event, building strength, pushing to go further, faster. I was just swimming because it felt nice, it felt playful, and I felt strong and supported.

It wasn't instant. I needed to work with temperature, experiment with clothing and timing. One thing that helped was 'habit-stacking' – a process recommended by James Clear in his book, *Atomic Habits*. For years I had a strong morning routine of stretches and mindfulness meditation. I just added swimming to the mix. My competitive nature helped because once I had a few weeks of daily swimming under my belt, I didn't want to ruin my streak!

Swimming enables me to listen to the language of my body. Held and supported in the water, I feel the rise and fall of gentle foot flopping kicks, water rushing through open palms, drips splashing my face. Even on high pain days, battling low energy and overwhelming emotions, mixing tears with salt water, I will still swim. It comforts me to know my family are close by, I look over at the house, smiling as I swim.

If I could go back to that exact moment that I decided I needed to push, please, prove and perform to win people's approval, I would draw my younger self onto my lap and whisper, 'Play, be silly, chase awe and wonder! That is a perfectly beautiful way to live your life. Don't blend in, don't push beyond what your body can do. Just be yourself. Your daggy, tortoise-paced, fun-loving self. You are perfect just as you are, little one.'

My daily swimming efforts have enabled me to live well with pain. There is no denying, it's been hard work. It takes time and effort, and the progress can be soul-crushingly slow. But the rewards are worth it. The pain is still there but it no longer consumes me.

Maybe swimming is not your thing. If you live with chronic pain, there are a myriad of other options for moving your own way. Something you know you can do that might shift the dial a little – a

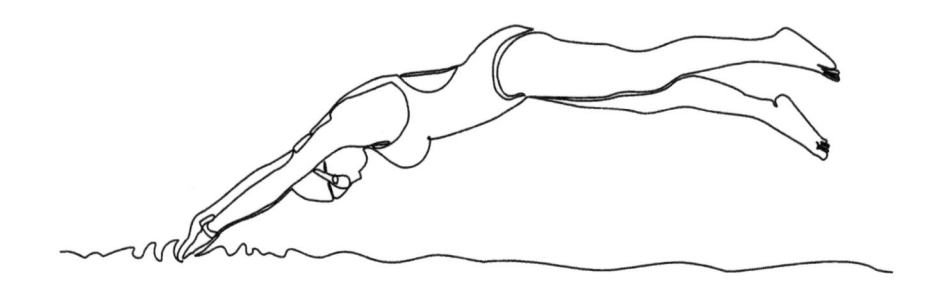

Swimming enables me to listen to the language of my body. Held and supported in the water, I feel the rise and fall of gentle foot flopping kicks, water rushing through open palms, drips splashing my face. Even on high pain days, battling low energy and overwhelming emotions, mixing tears with salt water, I will still swim.

little movement you can try or an act of self-compassion. While it can feel like everything is out of control, the way you move, the way you think and the way you feel are your puppet strings to command. Every time I push off from the wall, I am reminded of the strength within me.

This is my wish for you, dear reader. Through this, and the other stories in this book, may you find the courage and strength that you have within you. To follow your dream, whatever way works for you, step by step, stroke by stroke, breath by breath, go make your splash. One day, you might find you are fully engaged, in flow. Somehow, that thing you are doing has stopped being a chore or a requirement – and it has become your way of living.

Chapter Nine

Take It Easy

Growing up in Bangladesh, Shah Rafayat Chowdhury would turn to his father for advice and always received the same three-word answer. Today, Shah is an award-winning social entrepreneur and environmentalist – and it's all thanks to his father's favourite catchphrase.

'Take it easy.' Three simple words. Yet, these three simple words have had a profound impact on my life, whether it be in a situation where I was feeling anxious about exams, uncertain about work or even during times of great difficulty and heartache. These three words were magic for me; instantly calming me down, no matter how dire the situation was. 'Take it easy,' my father would say, and the entire world would come to a standstill, giving me the time to take a breath and come back to my centre.

As you'll read, I've faced many challenges in my life, including the death of my dad from pancreatic cancer. Even in my darkest moments, those three little words have had the power to reset and soothe me, and to give me an instant connection to my father – even after he was gone.

To understand the impact of that phrase, you first need to understand my childhood. I grew up in Dhaka, the capital of Bangladesh. When other children looked up to Superman and Batman as their role models, I looked up to Captain Planet – and there was a good reason for that. Captain Planet's main task was to protect the environment from evil, and in many ways, this superhero and my dad were similar.

My dad spent his entire life fighting against governments and large corporations to safeguard the environment for future generations. He fearlessly spoke up, even when the odds were against him. I remember him travelling around the world, never taking a break, in pursuit of environmental justice. My father was my own Captain Planet. It didn't take me long to work out what I wanted to be when I grew up: I wanted to fight for what was right, for the people and the environment, just like my father.

Despite his determination and powerful vision, my father was known as a kind, calm and lighthearted person. In his professional setting, he was called 'the little giant' – he wasn't a very tall person, but his voice held a certain gravitas that influenced people's decisions and actions, even those high up in government. Family, friends and colleagues knew him for his catchphrases. Whenever someone asked him how he was doing, he would respond with one of two comments: 'first class' or 'excellent'. In a complex and challenging world, such simple words reminded people that everything would be okay. I always admired how my father could do such hard and often heavy work, whilst remaining so positive and light.

I often reflect on how my mother was the complete opposite of him – extremely emotional. Maybe that is why my parents were a match made in heaven, striking a balance between two different personalities and ways of moving through the world. Growing up, I never saw them fight. My father's simple words seemed to have the power to calm her instantly too. Of course, there have been moments of crisis which tested us as a family, but my father always managed to steer the ship with his three simple words: 'Take it easy.'

Maybe you can think of a phrase that has guided your life – an affirmation that can instantly bring you home to yourself. For some people, it will be a sentence uttered by a parent, a sibling or a partner. For others, it will be a mantra which you've discovered has the power to soothe, realign or inspire. We whisper these words to ourselves in the middle of the night, when we're walking into an intimidating meeting or, as I discovered later, when we face losing someone who we love.

When I was a teenager, I remember struggling with anxiety before exams. I had a worry in my head: *What if I don't do well enough?* As a result, one phrase constantly circulated in my mind: *My life will be ruined.* With this mindset, study became even harder. At the time, my father was working in London and, knowing how emotional I was regarding the exams, he wrote me a letter and sent it all the way to Dhaka. In it, he wrote a paragraph that I still hold close to my heart:

Life is like a dancing down river. It takes a lot of curves and turns, as it is not always a straight line. If you have strong morale, great principle and firm determination, it is your world. I have to catch a flight now, so take it easy, my son. The world is yours for the taking, only if you believe in it without a doubt.

When I read my father's words, my mental burdens instantly lifted. I swapped the negative phrase, *My life will be ruined,* with his positive words, *Take it easy, my son.* With a more hopeful mindset, I was able to do well in the exams. Receiving that heartfelt paragraph from my father was a pivotal moment for me. It sparked a change in how I approached life from that point forward.

Growing up in Bangladesh, there is a lot of pressure on young people to become doctors, lawyers or engineers. I decided to be a maverick and do something different. At the age of seventeen, while in high school, I started my own non-profit – an organisation with

Despite his determination and powerful vision, my father was known as a kind, calm and lighthearted person. In his professional setting, he was called 'the little giant' – he wasn't a very tall person, but his voice held a certain gravitas that influenced people's decisions and actions, even those high up in government.

big aspirations to eradicate extreme poverty from the world through the design and creation of technological solutions to social and environmental problems.

This idea met the disapproval of many people. I remember teachers expressing their concern that I was choosing a career path and a life that was not as lavish as other professions. My friends made derogatory jokes that I would become a farmer when I grew up. What does a seventeen-year-old know about non-profits? Why would he choose this career path above other more respected careers? Whilst I did not have any experience or expertise, I did have two other important qualities – the passion to help the world and the dream of becoming like my father.

In the very early days of creating my not-for-profit, I had many doubts. I often wondered, *Do I have it in me to chase this dream?* In search for clarity, I decided to talk to my father. Dad had always dreamed that I would work for the United Nations and contribute to the environment at a global level. As I sat down to chat with him, I thought he would be against the idea of the grassroots not-for-profit. But, to my surprise, while I was telling him about my passions and my plans, he just kept on smiling. In fact, he was glowing. Dad ended the conversation with one phrase: 'Let others say what they want to say. You are my son, so do what you love and show the world what you can do.' Dad saw my potential, and helped me see it within myself. I never questioned my dream after that conversation.

As you can tell, my father, and his honest and encouraging words, are my North Star. So, you can imagine my shock when, in 2020, he had a major heart attack at the age of sixty. My father was fit and healthy – his diet and exercise regime put our family to shame. His heart attack sent disbelief through our family and a feeling of unease.

I remember being on the phone to my friend who knew a renowned cardiologist, begging him to arrange an appointment for my father. I kept saying the same words over and over again: 'Save my dad, please, save my dad, please.' I prayed to God to keep my father alive, so that he could witness the work I did with his own eyes, and smile with pride. During that moment, I learnt something about myself – my purpose in life was not only to help people overcome their hardships, but also to make my father proud. A big portion of my happiness was defined by his acknowledgement of me. I was chasing his approval, all this time – it was the drive within me.

Thankfully, God listened to my pleas. My father had open-heart surgery and it was a success. From that moment onward, I threw myself into my work. I worked around the clock to make my charitable work impactful. In the span of three years, my small non-profit impacted over 100,000 lives. We launched four new core programs. We received national and international awards and recognitions for our grassroots work. We became known as one of the fastest growing non-profits in the world, and one of the promising ones to come out of Bangladesh.

Every time we hit a new milestone, the first person I would tell or call would be my father. And his answers would always be the same, 'Excellent, my son, congratulations.' All it took was this one line to make my day. I was living my dream – making a positive impact and making my dad proud. Sadly, this dual sense of happiness was short-lived.

In early 2023, my father was diagnosed with late-stage pancreatic cancer. We did everything possible, but the doctors said there was nothing left to do. He only had a short time to live. In that moment I felt like I had failed my dad. I beat myself up for succeeding professionally but not personally. My father would never see me get married, have kids and start my own family – and that hurt. I started to question my life choices and wonder if I had chosen the right path.

Even at the end of his life, my father somehow understood my inner turmoil and what I was going through. One day when I went to visit him in hospital, with a weak voice, he asked me to sit beside him. He held my hand shakily, and he repeated those three magical words: 'Take it easy.' My father was so compassionate and strong that, even in the face of death, he could provide words of reassurance to his loved one.

From that moment, I did 'take it easy' – on myself, my life choices and my grief. In the final weeks of his life, I remember lying on the couch beside his bed, sharing ideas, philosophies and my dreams for the future. I asked him endless questions about his life and childhood. I wanted more words from the man of few words. When he became so weak that he couldn't talk anymore, I carried on the conversation and he nodded every now and then.

At one point, I told him that I wanted to be a writer one day and share my stories, experiences and emotions with the world. He gently nodded and told me to write a story about him. At the time, I thought it would be decades before I accomplished it, but here I am, one year after his death doing just that. The universe surely has a way of putting things into play fast.

When my father died in May 2023, there was a lot of emotion that night amidst my family – sadness, grief, shock. Through it all, I kept his words in my head like a soothing affirmation: 'Take it easy.' Those three little words, once again, reminded me that even in the hardest of times, that it would all be okay. Even in his death, he was there to help me.

The day after his death, I buried my father with my own hands, holding him one last time before putting him to rest eternally. But, oddly enough, it did not feel like I had completely lost him. His words, his teachings and the way he made me feel all remained in my mind, as clear and fresh as ever.

It has been a year since I lost my father, but never a day goes by where his words don't echo in my heart, encouraging me to continue

From that moment, I did 'take it easy' – on myself, my life choices and my grief. In the final weeks of his life, I remember lying on the couch beside his bed, sharing ideas, philosophies and my dreams for the future. I asked him endless questions about his life and childhood. I wanted more words from the man of few words.

to fight for justice and change. To date, my not-for-profit, Footsteps Bangladesh, has supported over 600,000 people to break through cycles of poverty, creating an example of building resilience for last mile communities across Bangladesh.

These days, I keep my father's legacy alive by teaching my staff to approach our work with a sense of calmness and lightheartedness. I try to make others feel that despite the complex challenges we face, everything will be alright. When my team goes through a tricky situation with a project or when communicating with donors and partners, I find myself automatically saying those three words, 'Take it easy.' Perhaps I have adopted my father's favourite catchphrase, allowing his words to live through mine in this current phase of time.

As for becoming a father myself one day, well, I hope this happens. And when it does, I'll be ready to offer my kids those three magic words.

As I finish writing this chapter, I can feel my emotions trying to burst out of my body, but I also hear a calming voice in my head that whispers, *Take it easy, my son. Everything will be okay.*

And once again I feel calm.

To find out more about Shah's innovate work responding to social and environmental challenges across Bangladesh, visit: *footstepsbd.org*.

Chapter Ten

Fear Less

Software engineer Gregory Murray was being treated for anxiety and depression when his medication gave him an unexpected side effect – fearlessness. After it ended, he kept fear from overwhelming him through the practices of improv, meditation and mindful self-compassion. This led him to poetry.

What would you do if you had no fear? What would you create if you had no fear of judgement from others or from yourself? Pause here and close your eyes. Reimagine your life without fear. I'll wait … What turned up for you? If you'll indulge me, write an email to yourself with the things you would do if the foreclosing fear was gone. Title the email *I love you*. Trust me. It's surprisingly powerful to receive those words from yourself.

What's that? You're curious what I would do if I had no fear? Thank you for asking! Let's just say that I have an unusual answer to that question.

In 2011, spring rains had raised forth a sea of bluebonnets across the empty fields of Austin, Texas, where I lived. With much-needed water falling on the outside, on the inside I had fallen into a deep, dry well of depression. I was drained of energy and self-confidence. I was constantly afraid of being exposed as an imposter after working for sixteen years as a software engineer with two liberal arts degrees. I had trouble falling and staying asleep. My mind would race like a car around a circular track of repetitive thoughts. All I could think about was work.

At the time, I was forty-three years old. My caring wife took me to a doctor to finally get the help I needed to address my lifelong struggle with social anxiety and depression. Her loving insistence had overcome my resistance to admit that I needed help for my mental 'weakness'. She had untied male culture's straitjacket from behind. Before long, I was taking antidepressants. My mind had stopped racing, but now I was moving slowly, overcome by brain fog.

Struggling to function in this clouded mental state, I spun the wheel to try a different combination of medications. I heard the click of the safe. I stepped out into a different world. I was not my usual self. Could this be my true, authentic self? All my fears were gone. I was no longer weighed down with the baggage of imposter syndrome, insecurity or regret. I was weightless and for the first time in decades, everything felt easy.

It was as if I had sent my harsh inner critic on a vacation. That guy was way too tense and needed a holiday from all the energy expended every day to keep me safe from everything. Psst, I didn't tell him it was a one-way trip to an island with no internet or cell phone service.

I slept and when I awoke, there was no dreading the day. I remember jumping out of bed, a circus song playing in my head. The world was a playground with no strict authority figure to say, 'Recess is over,' or, in my case, 'There is no recess because you don't deserve it.' My inner child was free and full of energy. I went from never dancing to dancing like a teenage girl, according to my wife. I'm certain she meant it as a compliment.

During this time, I became quite mischievous. Driving past a pet store, a thought came to me, I'd play a trick on my wife. I had always wanted to adopt an Australian sheep dog, but it was impractical with our small yard. So, I called my wife and left her a message pretending that I had adopted a four-legged friend and named him Skittles. I got really into this game, I even pretended that he was jumping on me as I left the message, 'Good boy, Skittles,' I said. My wife called me back and it quickly became apparent that she didn't think any of this was funny. I felt lighter, younger and more carefree than I had in years.

I excitedly told my doctor I was the poster child for an anti-anxiety medication. Witnessing the dramatic transformation of my personality, he fell back on his heels with a look of shock. It was as if he was saying to himself: *What have I done?* Later on, I would be diagnosed with bipolar II disorder brought on by a drug-induced hypomania. This rare disorder differs from the psychotic mania experienced in bipolar I that requires hospitalisation. Hypomania is characterised by a cheerful, euphoric mood, and a dramatic increase in self-confidence, talkativeness and energy. People with it experience increased goal-directed activity, disinhibited behaviour and amplified creativity.

I was strangely comforted by the diagnosis as it accurately described how I was feeling – free from the weight of judgement and self-doubt and fuelled by a new experience of overflowing hypercreativity. I only needed to look at our dining table for evidence. It was covered with storyboards I'd made for a movie I was directing for a work contest. I wrote a poem for the first time since first grade.

Spring Forward!
When flower buds peel
A smile breaks upon her face
A welcome release from winter's embrace

A flirting glance from her shoulders
Oh, to feel, to trace
Vivid hues in life's endless race

I moved from the fear of rejection to rejecting fear. I started taking improv classes and my creativity expanded even more. In improv there is no script. You approach a scene with a mindset to just 'be average'. This quietened the distracting, running commentary of my inner perfectionist. You can't be planning what to say as your partner is talking (sound familiar?) since the flow is swift and unpredictable. Instead, with improv you tap into your intuitive mind by saying the first thing that comes to you. We listen, hanging on every word, we accept our partner's gift of the next step in the storyline and add to it by saying, in essence, 'Yes, and' rather than 'Yes, but'. Together, we create something unexpected and beautiful. If the story veers off the road, we have the option to slide out of the clown car, bow and proudly say, 'I have failed' to a standing ovation from our fellow improvisers.

Amazingly, I began to take these lessons out into my everyday life. I noticed I was more present for my family, less distracted by repetitive thoughts, and had more ideas to share. In the before times, my manager at work would frequently have to call upon me in meetings. Now, at one meeting my manager told me to, 'Just shut up!' With my total personality change, my wife was not only worried about me adopting a dog but also about me getting fired. All the while I thought I would get a promotion.

My reading speed doubled as I drank in non-fiction works to fill up my reservoir of knowledge. My verbal fluency was a flood. To my surprise, pleasant memories were coming back, ones I couldn't access when my inner critic was on guard. My senses opened. I tasted those fruity notes they put on wine labels. I said to myself, *So this is what it's like to be human?*

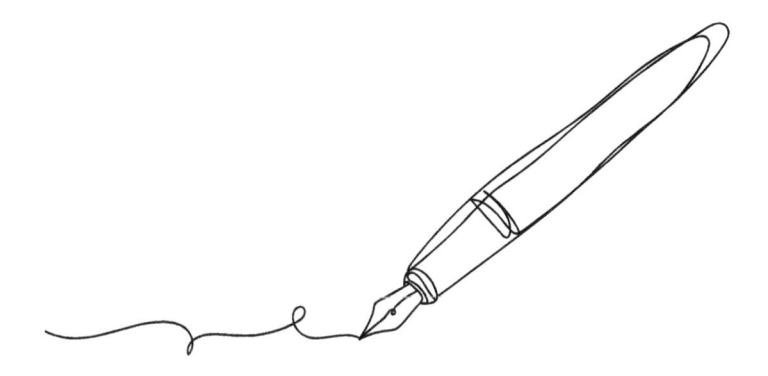

I was strangely comforted by the diagnosis as it accurately described how I was feeling – free from the weight of judgement and self-doubt and fuelled by a new experience of overflowing hypercreativity.

I became so confident in the 'new me' that one night I decided I didn't need to take a sleeping pill before bed. To my shock, I woke up in the morning to discover that I had returned to my former self. I had come back down to Earth. My inner critic had returned from his 'vacation' – and he was pissed. He reimposed hyperdiscipline and swept away the glitter of hypercreativity.

I tried everything to get back to that feeling of confidence and hypercreativity. But instead of freedom, the different medication combinations resulted in a roller-coaster of emotions, mood swings and harsh words to my wife. One time our ten-year-old son stood silently, holding up a piece of paper with the single word, *Why?* Frankly, it got pretty dark for a while as I went to some places I hope you never have to go. But eventually, my mood stabilised, and I began to accept my new 'imperfect' reality.

Every day, more and more people are being prescribed medication for anxiety, depression, neurodivergence, chronic pain and so on. Desperate for a quick fix, we can be lured into getting that prescription filled for ourselves or those we love. Whilst my story of getting bipolar II as a side effect of medication is statistically rare, riding the waves of medication and trying to get the dosage right is something many of us will experience over the course of our lives. We owe it to ourselves and those around us to be educated about side effects and other ways we can learn to soothe and enliven ourselves, befriend our inner critic and manage our thoughts.

That period in my life taught me many things. Most significantly, it revealed to me that every day I have a choice. I can pause and ask myself: *What would my fearless self do in this moment?* And so, for the next decade, I asked myself this question regularly. Whilst it didn't crack the code and reopen the safe to hypercreativity, it changed my life in more subtle and sustainable ways. I haven't always gotten it right, but I've kept on asking. One time I drove to an improv class and turned around halfway there as fear got the better of me. Another time, I made it all the way to the class and thoroughly enjoyed myself.

I was taking consistent steps in the right direction. Then one day, by chance, I took a leap towards meditation. They were running a free session at work, so I gave it a try. The meditation teacher mentioned she was going to be facilitating an eight-week mindful self-compassion course on the weekends. Despite my inner critic arguing the opportunity cost of not using that time to learn for work, I signed up, paid and told my teacher I would be there. During this course, one of my core beliefs was challenged. I'd spent my entire life thinking that being hard on myself was the only way to achieve things and be successful. Over eight weekends, I learnt that self-compassion is a better strategy than inner criticism. It helps us break our fall and our fear of trying.

My teachers read poetry. I was inspired. They said we could bring something to share on the last day of class. I thought about writing a poem, but it was fifty-fifty whether I would just work on the weekend as usual. That was until I realised the opportunity to give my teachers a gift would never come again. I used the lessons from improv to write the first thing that came to mind without fear or hesitation. Here are a few lines.

may you live with ease
the ease of knowing
that you, you are enough

With improv, meditation and self-compassion as my allies, over the coming months, something shifted within me. For so long, my inner critic had made me focus on efficiency. I had to quickly shore up my weaknesses before others found out that I was an imposter. There was no time for exploration. Everything was viewed through the lens of how it would be useful for work, blurring everything else to the background. But now, I was beginning to see the benefits of creativity without it having to be useful for work. I was exploring because it felt good.

I began to wake early and jump out of bed to write poetry. Here's a sampling.

We can spend time full of regrets
wishing for a better past
We can spend time anxious
about what never comes to pass

We may spend our precious time remaining
in between past and future
with all of our senses ablazing
seeing the world anew
from a child's point of view

A positive, upwards cycle had begun to replace decades of spiralling downwards. A friend told me my poem inspired him during his recovery from a stroke. I gifted a poem to a teacher navigating a challenging time. A poem was even published in a book. I felt like I was making a contribution beyond work. All of this began by asking the simple question: *What would my fearless self do in this moment?*

But as with all habits, they require strategies to make them stick. Want to consume less social media? Try removing the apps from your home screen. Want to eat more healthy foods? Place them front and centre. Want to go to the gym more frequently before work? Try putting your clothes for work in your gym bag the night before and only shower at the gym. Once you arrive you can tell yourself, *Now that I'm here, I can at least exercise for twenty minutes.* As they say, 80% of life is showing up.

That period in my life taught me many things. Most significantly, it revealed to me that every day I have a choice. I can pause and ask myself: What would my fearless self do in this moment? And so, for the next decade, I asked myself this question regularly.

As I've integrated the habit of writing poetry into my life, I've reminded myself of two things. The first is the importance of developing an enjoyable routine around our habits. Our brains are expensive to operate and account for an outsized 20% of the energy our bodies use during the day. There is comfort in routine and ritual from the ease of not spending extra energy having to decide. We all know that willpower can be ineffective in making a habit stick, as we burn cognitive energy in fighting ourselves, and burn ourselves out. As I discovered, we are more likely to continue a practice if we make the routine surrounding it comforting and pleasing. That's why my poetry routine includes making a delicious cup of coffee and taking a moment to enjoy the aroma rising from the silky espresso beans before I write.

For me, the second aspect of successful habit creation is accepting setbacks. Doing something every day ties into the power of loss aversion, of not wanting to stop a streak. But life will happen, spilling that same coffee over all our plans (or poems), almost as if they were knocked over by a darting Aussie sheep dog named Skittles. When interruptions happen, we can become defeated thinking that they will happen again, so why keep trying? Research shows that if we allow ourselves two emergency passes a week, we are more resilient when interruptions inevitably happen. As I experimented with these emergency passes on the mornings I didn't wake up and write poetry before work, I realised they were a version of self-compassion. I began to forgive rather than berate myself for breaking my winning streak. I reframed these setbacks as a chance for a fresh start. Just as I had learnt to come back gently when my mind wandered in meditation, I learnt to come back to my poetry with the same tenderness and ease.

I wonder if as you read this you are smiling, seeing yourself in my story. Is there a part of you that gets cross with yourself when you break your winning streak? Perhaps you could benefit from allowing yourself the occasional emergency pass too? Or would creating a more pleasant ritual around your habits help?

I've travelled to the depths of depression and the highs of hypercreativity, and I've landed somewhere in-between. Now, I know my two feet are on the ground and I'm in a place where I feel like I am enough. Through improv, meditation, self-compassion and poetry I'm filling in the pages of my memory passport with the stamps of new experiences, creations and connections. I feel excited for what's to come.

We can't always be fearless, but with practice, we can change our minds to fear less. You can do this. I'm rooting for you. Now read the email you sent yourself entitled *I love you* or go and write it now. Like improv, you can start anytime, anywhere to create your life's story.

Chapter Eleven

Show Me the Way

As a recovering perfectionist, Lisa Benson had spent her entire life trying to control outcomes and other people's opinions – until she embraced a 'secret' spiritual habit, which had been speaking to her since her childhood.

'The bird has the answer.' The words didn't make sense, but they were simple and succinct, cutting through the deep silence of the night. It was 2020, amid the uncertainty of the pandemic. Although it's been a few years now, I still hear the words as if they are being whispered in my ear today.

At the time, I was forty-five years old, a full-time writer and newly married – but something was niggling. I had been writing a memoir about my life, exploring the ways that my lifelong perfectionism and need to be seen as a 'good girl' had stopped me from living fully. If you've ever explored your childhood conditioning, you'll know that it's a powerful process but can leave you feeling a little … untethered.

One night, as I lay in my bed, I found myself asking a series of questions, sending them out to the universe: *Where am I meant to go from here?* and *Please help guide me what to do next.* The *'pleeease'* was stretched to capacity like a rubber band. I was seeking answers, and I wanted to know *now*.

As I heard, 'The bird has the answer,' I sat up in bed and opened my eyes, scanning the faint shards of moonlight that decorated the walls of my bedroom. Who said that? What on Earth does it mean? What bird? My husband was sound asleep beside me. I remember being curious at the time how slow my heart was beating. Was this a direct communication from my spirit guides? I was confident it wasn't my imagination.

Whilst the mysterious message didn't make sense, it did initiate a change within me. On a daily, or at least weekly basis I began asking for guidance from something bigger than me, and my usual circle of confidantes. I stopped searching for answers on my Facebook feed or in 'expert' articles. Instead, I began to confide in a group of 'spirit guides', connect with angels and trust my own spiritual intuition at last.

If this all sounds very 'woo-woo', I get it. By this point, I had been meditating on and off for about twenty-five years, and as I said, I was writing my memoir and diving deep into my past, but this was the first time I'd heard my consciousness (or whatever it was!) talking back to me so clearly. It was certainly a detour from the beliefs of my childhood and the decades of trying to please others and hide the real me.

When I was a child, I had been sceptical of many things, including religion. Even though both of my parents grew up in religious households, I'd heard them speak about how they stopped attending Sunday church services at eighteen, when it became their own choice. So, when I grew curious about spirituality during my high school years, I felt the need to keep it a secret. I understand that spirituality and religion aren't the same, but as a young girl, it seemed all things unexplainable or categorised as *woo-woo* were taboo.

Growing up, Mum hung washing on the line with same-coloured

pegs and cut food into exact cubes (discarding the odd shaped offcuts). Everything in our family home was in size, or alphabetical, order which prompted my sister and I to 'daughter diagnose' Mum with OCD (obsessive compulsive disorder). Keeping my doll's hair in pristine condition even though I longed to brush it, and returning games into their original packaging, meant there was no place for chit-chatting with invisible friends.

Spirituality to me now, is the energetic and vibrational trust in something beyond myself, connecting me to every other soul on this planet (and beyond). It is a sense that we are not confined by our 'third-dimensional reality'. It's about connection with whoever, or whatever feels aligned to each of us, whether it's the universe, God, higher beings or spirit. Some people may not believe in anything that cannot be scientifically proven or physically seen. That's fine too. But my experiences have given me faith that something else does exist and this brings me comfort, so it's right for me, for now.

My fascination with higher beings – the invisible link beyond life as we experience it – wasn't an attempt to follow a spiritual trend. It was an inner knowing that had me searching for something 'extra' from a very young age. My earliest memory of metaphysical beings was in primary school. My friend Cassandra and I would head for the trees in the barked area where we would live out our fantasy world with the 'fairies', which would play in the palms of our hands. Unlike the voice in the night, this experience was more likely my imagination running wild – I am mindful of the difference. But it was a fun introduction to spiritual beings.

As I got older, I craved knowledge and was curious about esoteric things. Walking into my teenage room at my parents' home was like stepping into a spiritual cave adorned with mobiles, angels, tealight candles and crystals. A Native American dreamcatcher was positioned above my bed to whoosh away my bad dreams. In the early nineties when everything 'new age' was popular, I was in my element. I'd spend hours in my favourite spiritual shop, breathing in the energy (and incense), while reading the back blurbs on the books I planned to buy with future pays from my after-school job.

It's hard to believe that such a bright and curious teenager would spend the next two decades 'settling' and 'pleasing' others. A smart girl wouldn't accept a mediocre life … would she? During my late twenties and early thirties, I lost connection with my inner spark. All my energy had been depleted from putting up with dysfunction in relationships. I became an expert at filtering my words, appeasing insecure men and wearing uncomfortable G-strings to bed because my boyfriend considered it 'sexy'. I know, I know. Who puts up with such crap?

At the time, no-one in my inner circle would have expected me to converse with spirits. It would have been as foreign as making a phone call to Santa Claus. So, I closed that part of myself off. I didn't tell anyone about the premonitions I had (how I dreamt I broke a limb and that a friend was made redundant, before these incidents actually happened) in case people thought 'I was making them up'.

All this changed when my dad died. I was thirty-six years old and finally, parts of me that had been asleep for too long woke up. After Dad passed away, I witnessed streetlights come on and off as I drove under them (the same light at different times), and several times I walked into my home to hear the television on, which had never happened before his death. I have since learned that it's common for spirits to communicate through electricity. The day before Dad passed, I made a promise to him to live more authentically. 'He won't be here for much longer,' I'd announced, referring to my long overdue intention to leave a toxic partner. Was Dad trying to let me know he approved of the break-up from another realm? It gives me goosebumps to think that this man who outwardly dismissed spirituality may be the very proof it exists.

Do we all receive messages? Personally, I believe we do, especially children and animals as they're less 'closed down' and more open to receiving them. Some of us accept that higher beings are interacting with us, while others only see freaky coincidences. I didn't curate any of the things. I wasn't forcing myself to see or hear anything. They just happened.

Are our habits even planned, or do the ones we truly embody emerge organically? Sometimes it's impossible to trace where a pattern originally formed. If we try to force a habit – like typical new year's resolutions – they often don't last. Our intellectual mind breeds '*trying*' energy, whereas actions that emerge from the soul emanate '*being*' energy. There was never a time I wrote on my bucket list: *Make a habit to chat with invisible guides.* I believe the behaviours that form part of our identity are the ones we only recognise when we look back on our experiences.

While writing my memoir, *Where Have I Been all My Life?* I learned that authors often call in a muse to help them channel messages that are meant to be shared. I started burning palo santo and swooshing it around the room. Then I would sit on the floor cross-legged and do a short meditation to ground myself. I ended each meditation with the statement: 'Bring this book into my being.' I said it over and over as I struggled with the conditioning and healing I had to work through in order to write my memoir. The final line in my book's acknowledgements is, 'I am grateful to the universe for trusting this story in my hands. I asked you over and over to "bring this book into my being," and my wish was granted. Thank you.'

As I wrote my book, my need to be real far outweighed my desire for acceptance. Finally! The layers of conditioning began to fall, and I was ready to share my thoughts without being told what I 'should' say. My book about finding my voice had to be raw and authentic, or what was the point? I was guided to reveal my greatest vulnerabilities and

Are our habits even planned, or do the ones we truly embody emerge organically? Sometimes it's impossible to trace where a pattern originally formed. If we try to force a habit – like typical new year's resolutions – they often don't last. Our intellectual mind breeds 'trying' energy, whereas actions that emerge from the soul emanate 'being' energy.

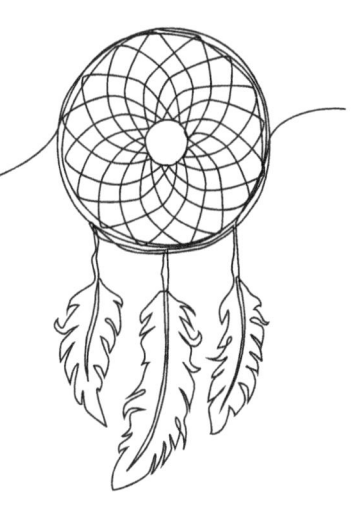

shames. I had to share the whole story, not just the shiny parts as if it were a social media post. Previously I had kept my story private, just like my relationship with spiritual beings. Today, whenever I write, I intentionally carry out my pre-writing ritual. I see myself as a conduit, communicating with greater universal energy.

I know many people reading this story will be sceptical of the messages I receive and the guidance I follow. I don't know what is best for you, but maybe hearing my story can help you recognise similar connections in your own life? You too may already be subconsciously communicating with your spirit guides without labelling it a habit or ritual. You may call on 'parking angels' when you are hoping for a free car space in a busy carpark, or asking an invisible source, *What am I supposed to do now?* It may be as simple as noticing angel numbers, like 11:11 on your phone, clock, the car's odometer or other places where number sequences change. Communicating with higher beings has helped lift the burden of control for me.

I always thought I had the power to direct my life, but it was only an illusion. Living most of my life seeking validation from others was overwhelming; trying to control other people's thoughts and how my life would turn out was time consuming and caused me health issues, including a chronic upset stomach and skin rashes. Following my dad's death, I realised I had less free will than I imagined, and my life is going to unfold however it is meant to – and this was a powerful step in my recovery from perfectionism.

My generation, Gen X, were conditioned to strive, but wouldn't it be more beneficial to teach the next generations to allow. Now that I'm a grandmother, I am already teaching our grandson how to meditate – and he's not even two. Of course, it's not for long, but he has the pose perfected and squeezes his little eyes closed when I do. He may not choose to continue this practice, but how progressive for him to be exposed to varied perspectives which reinforce more openness and less shame.

If you've never thought about communicating with spirit guides, you may begin to explore by getting comfortable in the silence of meditation – even if it's just five minutes a day. If that feels okay, you can extend the time, and begin to listen for guidance or set intentions by silently speaking your thoughts and concerns. If I'm overwhelmed I might say, *Calling in Archangel Haniel. Haniel, I need to relax more. Please guide me to things that will be helpful and bring me peace.* If that feels a little too spiritual, try connecting with your body to ask what it's trying to tell you. Our body is an amazing signpost, unmasking situations that are (and aren't) right for us and people in our life who enhance or damage our wellbeing. Or maybe it's as simple as voicing to others what you genuinely need, instead of allowing others direct your path. I know the pain of tumbleweeding though life in this way.

The answers don't come in the way we expect, and universal timing doesn't work on the same timeline as we are used to. Asking for answers is a practice that needs persistence and patience. It is also imperfect. I've had panic attacks during group meditations and been told by a hypnotherapist to declutter my (apparently too large) spiritual community. I laugh now, but I liken it to a piece of writing that needed editing down to discard the superfluous words.

I'm not going to proclaim I meditate and converse with spirit guides every day, but I do it most days because I feel better when I do. Instead of allowing the world around me to dictate my path, it helps me tune in to my soul which I know is where all the answers reside.

I've found healing in recognising we can't trust the universe until we have faith in ourselves. I choose to believe in higher beings because it brings comfort to me, and beyond that, it supports the belief that we are all connected to one another. I feel held and at peace, knowing there is something greater than me, guiding me on my path. I chose to stop keeping my ritual a secret – and to even 'out' it in this book – because

I've found healing in recognising we can't trust the universe until we have faith in ourselves.

I believe people need spirituality now more than ever. I want to share my experience in the hope you can benefit too. In a way, me going inward and having a personal relationship with my guides instead of doing what the world expects me to do is aligned with my personal progress. When I started trusting myself and asking for what *I* needed, the messages began to flow more freely. I had to get comfortable communicating better with my husband, family and friends and my reward was this deeper connection to higher beings.

I feel a strong calling to share my experiences through my writing. Even though I don't have my own children, I have grandchildren as a result of my husband's previous relationship. My DNA may not live on but my stories will. Receiving guidance and clarity for my thoughts, through my ritual of communicating with spirit guides, keeps the ripple going in an infinite future.

I am writing these words from a boat on a still autumn day, the lake mirroring the shoreline. I smile as I witness a symphony of bellbirds. I notice seagulls fly past, the odd eagle high in the sky, plus a variety of bird calls from the trees surrounding the bay where my husband and I have anchored our vessel.

Four years on, from that night when I received a message in my bed, I'm still not convinced I know which bird has the answer for me. Is it the barn owl that delivered the rings at our wedding? Is it the magpie that visits the balcony of our home? Is it one of the dozens of birds Dad bred when we were kids? Maybe there is a missing piece, where I haven't connected the relevance of a particular bird. Or maybe *the* bird hasn't presented itself in my life yet.

As I complete this chapter, I breathe a long expansive breath and close my eyes as I contemplate and surrender. I am finally at peace with not knowing all the answers. As long as I am open to this ongoing conversation, I trust I will be led in the direction I'm meant to go.

Chapter Twelve

Catching the Wind

Retired school principal Fred Locke has straddled two passions throughout his life – ballet and sailing. Whether dancing professionally in Europe or sailing across turbulent waters, his hobbies taught him one thing: to relish in the present moment.

'We are off to look at boats,' my dad and I would say to my mum at least once every summer during my childhood. My mum was happy to accommodate our boys' adventure, so long as 'look' was the operative word. This special bonding time for Dad and I often included hours admiring wooden boats. As we walked through the Concordia boat-building shop, we were both in awe of the craftsmanship, the colour palettes and the delightful smell of cedar wood. We always grabbed a hotdog for lunch and chatted about our next sailing adventure. During the winter months, I would send away for colour brochures of small cruising sailboats and dream of the day I could afford to buy one for myself.

I share my dad's passion for sailing and, in the tidal rivers of Westport Point, Massachusetts, he taught me well. I remember vividly letting go of the mooring buoy on my first solo sail with nerves flying. Heading off on a starboard tack, I grabbed the main and jib sheets, centreboard was down, and the sails filled – I was sailing! Short tacking through two mudflats to reach deeper water in the main channel was next, and I was all in. Sailing daily in Westport with friends – each in our own or family boats – buoyed confidence and camaraderie in my youth.

During my junior high years, a Philadelphia paper route helped me save money that my parents agreed to match, and at fifteen, I purchased a twelve-foot-four-inch wooden Concordia Beetle-Cat. She was thirty-five years old. I called her *Pertelotte*. Over the coming years, sailing offered opportunities that felt like a rite of passage. One time my friend Grog and I were becalmed at night as we attempted to sail to Martha's Vineyard off the Massachusetts coast. Enthusiastic, energetic and optimistic, we set off on a trip we imagined would take six hours. On this night the joy of sailing met the sobering reality of being totally at the mercy of the tidal current and no wind. Just two boys, a twelve-foot boat and darkness. Thankfully, the wind eventually picked up and with a new-found maturity and determination, we made it across safely, arriving at 2:30am, five hours after our ETA. I remember a group of seasoned sailors telling us our journey was less than wise and that we were lucky to have made it.

Sailing brings me great joy. The wind in your face, moving through the water, navigating tides and eddies and plotting your next move. It is a wonderful combination of fun, challenging and relaxing. Kenneth Graham, in *Wind in the Willows,* puts it this way: 'There is nothing – absolutely nothing – so much worth doing as simply messing about in boats.' No two days are alike; add company and pleasure arrives easily.

But sailing wasn't my only passion. Ever since I can remember, I have also loved to dance. I grew up square dancing, and at the age of nineteen, I discovered another unconventional hobby for a young man

– ballet. Introduced to ballet by friends, as a former athlete, I loved the physical challenge and moving to classical music.

When I told my parents that I wanted to learn ballet, they were supportive (although they initially thought dancing would be a passing phase). We talked about it, and in return for promising to finish college, my parents let me dance in New York City for one year. I loved the routine of taking classes and stretching. I was learning, following one of my passions and loving life. Unfortunately, serious tendonitis in both knees forced me to stop dancing. With sadness and frustration, I returned home and subsequently finished college earning a BA in history.

Determined not to let my dreams die, after graduating, I made the decision to study at The College of the Royal Academy of Dancing in London. Over the next three years, with the exception of another bout of tendonitis, I gradually became stronger, my dancing improved greatly and got my first professional dancing job in West Germany. I loved performing ballets, musicals like *Cabaret*, operas and operettas.

I enjoyed nineteen years of both performing and teaching dance. I travelled from Europe back to America and delighted in dancing character roles like Drosselmeyer in the *Nutcracker* and Lord Capulet and Friar Laurence in *Romeo and Juliet*. The ballet world is very competitive and disciplined; many ballet dancers are singularly focused on their 'craft'. For me, sailing provided some balance and a great respite. It allowed me to break away from needing to be 'perfect'. It gave me another identity when navigating injuries and setbacks that invariably punctuate the life of a professional dancer. Sailing was also a welcome vehicle for connection with my family over the many years I lived abroad. I can still remember opening the letters my parents would send me describing their sailing adventures. In those moments I could smell the salty ocean air and feel the wind on my face, even though I was thousands of miles away.

Looking back, there is a common thread in my life – connecting with people through shared hobbies and interests. Finding a love of sailing meant that I was instantly part of a community from a young age, whether it was bonding with my dad, my friends and, later, my sisters. Dance was a whole new world and gave me a way to express myself – an instant, emotional connector with other dancers and the audience. As performers we create magic and it is a wonderful way to give back. Rehearsing and performing is exhilarating and exhausting, and it is the nuanced refinement that makes the magic believable and fun. I'm curious, do you enjoy the social aspect of your interests or do you prefer solitude when immersed in your hobbies or passions?

So often in life we are forced to walk one path, to narrow down our interests and focus on one. I am grateful that I could juggle and relish both passions. Whilst different, both sailing and dancing helped me connect to the miracle that is my physical body. I learned to spend long periods of time in presence and flow and to respond well to changing circumstances. Perhaps reading my story has allowed you to see your diverse interests or passions with a fresh perspective. Or maybe you can recall a time when you were made to choose between two aspects of your life that you really enjoyed?

As with all passions, they change over time just as we do. Seeing both my daughters performing in the *Nutcracker* was as cool as performing myself. I felt so proud. The words of my previous artistic director 'there are no small parts' echoed in my mind and took on a new significance as I delighted in all the dancers on stage. Although dance was not something my children pursued professionally, I continued to perform *Nutcrackers* as they grew up, and the shared experience was bonding. When I stopped dancing and became a school principal in my forties (like my dad and grandfather), it was a delight to have sailing as it always offered me a healthy dose of nature and excitement.

I continued to sail with my dad well into his old age. These days

Looking back, there is a common thread in my life – connecting with people through shared hobbies and interests. Finding a love of sailing meant that I was instantly part of a community from a young age, whether it was bonding with my dad, my friends and, later, my sisters. Dance was a whole new world and gave me a way to express myself – an instant, emotional connector with other dancers and the audience.

I enjoy sailing with my sisters. We love going fast and don't mind getting wet. To make a Sunfish 'plane' like a windsurfer takes a perfect combination of wind angle, hiking out to keep the hull flat, absorbing the spray and hanging on. These moments are short-lived but glorious! It is so cool to be right on the edge. When the hull literally lifts out of the water and you are screaming along, there is nothing better! It is one aspect of sailing heaven.

Sometimes my sister and I laugh at how far we have come as a sailing team. We reminisce about the time I tried to teach her to sail, about fifty years prior. I was an energetic teenager who decided that the perfect birthday present for my youngest sister would be three sailing lessons. The first two were unmemorable. But on the third lesson, a sustained puff of wind meant that the boat took in water and my sister became very scared. Emotions were high. What was meant to be a fun bonding experience left my sister shaken and I was frustrated and disappointed.

At sixty-eight years old, I am retired and looking forward to the next chapter in my sailing story. The Columbia River, cruising in the beautiful San Juan Islands near Seattle, Washington, and exploring large lakes in Oregon and the surrounding north-west are all on my list. My current boat is a good size for me to eventually sail single-handed, and I plan to 'boat camp' with or without company.

At Christmas, I purchased an 'asymmetrical spinnaker', which is the large balloon-like sail used when wanting to sail well off the wind. Recently, I worked with a rigger to purchase and install the additional winches, lines and hardware needed for this specific sail. Learning to correctly and safely fly this sail is a steep learning curve that I am looking forward to. With practice, my goal is to use this sail with company, including my daughters, grandchildren and friends. Fortunately, with retirement, I have time.

What I've learnt from my 'life of distinct passions' is, you can give

So often in life we are forced to walk one path, to narrow down our interests and focus on one. I am grateful that I could juggle and relish both passions. Whilst different, both sailing and dancing helped me connect to the miracle that is my physical body.

yourself the freedom to not have to choose. If you took me back to my teenage days and asked me to choose between dance and sailing, it would have been a very tough call, and I would probably have picked sailing. But, in doing so, I would have robbed myself of so many amazing opportunities, connections and experiences. If you are a parent, grandparent, teacher or friend, I hope you'll encourage the young people in your life to explore multiple passions so that they can grow into adults with diverse skills, experiences, talents and ideas.

Life is hopefully long and, if you're lucky, you'll have the chance to explore the land and the sea, and to express yourself in many ways. As I would say to my former students at graduation, 'Dream big, work hard and enjoy!'

Chapter Thirteen

Choosing Love Over Fear

Raised in a fundamentalist Pentecostal church within a belief system that instilled fear, Christey West grew up feeling unsafe in a dangerous world – until she found her own ways to connect with the divine.

It was time to worship the Lord. I was ten years old, standing in my local Pentecostal church that I attended every Sunday morning in the suburbs of Christchurch, New Zealand, surrounded by a congregation of early-nineties hairdos and brightly coloured blazers. Believers were closing their eyes and lifting their hands, one by one, to praise Jesus.

A woman on the right of the aisle started 'speaking in tongues' as people around me were moved to tears by their experiences. In those days, I was regularly told that Jesus lived in my heart, but I wasn't really sure what that meant. I couldn't feel him there like everyone else seemed to.

It was a new song on the projector that day and I didn't know the lyrics. Seeking proof that God existed, as I often did, I closed my eyes and earnestly prayed, *If you're real, let me sing the right words of the song without needing to read them. Amen.* It didn't work – I didn't magically know the words.

So, I sent the Holy Spirit a different request: give me the gift of speaking in tongues. After a while, I quietly started to speak: '*Ahh kalamachika kuuchi kuuchi …*' It came out but I knew I was just twisting my tongue and making new sounds. I stopped in case the family worshipping next to me heard and found me ridiculous.

It was a special church service that Sunday. There was a visiting pastor who had flown all the way from America to 'lay hands' on the people of Christchurch. People around me were moving to the front of the church, lining up to receive 'more of God'. I decided to give it a go – partly because staying in my seat might make people question my salvation.

The pastor prayed over people, in tongues and in English, his anointed hands hovering over their foreheads. One by one I watched women, men and some children become filled with the Holy Spirit until they fainted. Catchers stood behind each person, placing them gently on the ground as they fell.

My turn was coming up. I wondered, excitedly, how it was going to feel to be so filled with Jesus that I passed out. The pastor put his hand over my forehead and started praying for me. I closed my eyes and waited, bursting with anticipation. Some time passed and he leaned in closer to me, praying louder, so I leaned back to adjust the space between us. He leaned forward again, and my stomach muscles engaged as I leaned back further.

I wasn't filled with anything except wonder – at why the pastor kept pushing me backwards. His hand was touching my forehead now and my abs started to hurt. It got awkward. I sensed he wanted me to fall over so we could all save face. Considering I was overbalancing anyway I let myself fall into the catcher's eager arms and I lay on the ground with everyone else.

'Hallelujah!' the pastor proclaimed. 'Praise Jesus.'

Have you ever felt like you were the only one in the room who didn't get it, but you desperately wanted to see what everyone else could see? This was often my experience throughout my fundamentalist Christian upbringing. But on top of the confusion and doubt there was a much darker emotion that characterised those years: fear. Or maybe 'terror' is more accurate.

Growing up, I received scary and conflicting messages. I was taught that if your heart wasn't 'right with Jesus' when you died, you'd be tortured by terrifying demons for eternity. And while you're alive, if you doubt anything written in the Bible it's because demons have possessed your mind and are trying to lead you to the devil. 'But you have no reason to fear!' the adults assured me. 'Just plead the blood of Jesus and the demons will flee.' I don't know what 'pleading the blood of Jesus' means now and I certainly didn't as a child.

I spent much of my childhood seeking God and looking for evidence that he existed. It wasn't until I was fifteen years old that I finally received some proof, and my direct line to the divine opened up.

It was a hot summer's day, and I was on holiday in New Zealand's scenic South Island, playing tennis badly with a family friend, Stephanie. The tennis court was semi-abandoned, and wild nature was reclaiming the land for itself, growing through the cracks in the old concrete and rusty wire fencing. It was located next to a shallow, pretty river.

Stephanie and I had worked up a sweat, so we decided to cross the river and cool off. We were oblivious to the fact that the river was connected to a dam that periodically released torrents of water. When we were halfway across the river, the current suddenly sped up and started pushing us downstream. We tried to hold hands to balance but the rushing water separated us. Stephanie managed to get safely to the other side before the dam released a flood of ferocious water that swept me clean off my feet. The water suddenly became very deep, forcing me underwater, swirling and twirling.

When the current finally pushed me back up to the surface, I gasped a breath before being thrust into the riverbank. I tried to grab onto the bank, but the shingle was too dusty and loose to grip. The current swiftly pulled me back under. *So, this is how I die,* I thought. Out of options, my heart sent out an SOS I had learned in church: *Save me, Jesus!*

I came up to the surface again and caught a breath as I was rammed into the riverbank for a second time. I knew there was no way I could grip onto the loose shingle, but I had nothing to lose so I reached my hand out – somehow, my hand stuck to the earth. I tried my other hand and it stuck too! Then, with no effort at all, one hand after the other, I lifted myself out of the crazed river, as if someone was gently pushing me up from below.

I stood on the riverbank in complete shock. The world stopped moving as it sank in that I was free from the river – and still alive! In that moment I knew without a doubt that a supernatural force had saved me. Jesus, or some inexplicable entity that was much more powerful than me, existed.

Unfortunately, this validation didn't make life as an Evangelical Christian any more meaningful to me. I had nothing against Jesus but the controlling, fearful environment in church that shamed and judged and threatened didn't feel very heavenly. Eighteen years of Sunday services hadn't provided me with the promised inner peace. So, the week after high school finished, I moved out of home and stopped going to church.

I spent a lot of the next decade travelling. During this time, I met and learnt from people with a variety of beliefs. To my surprise, the Buddhists, Muslims and Hindus that I met weren't possessed by the devil. And I discovered warm, loving Christians who didn't want to

You don't need to have had a near-death experience or to have grown up in a religious setting to believe that life can be mysterious. Perhaps for you this something 'more' is synchronicity, awe and wonder, or unconditional love.

control my life. I also encountered humanitarian atheists and insightful Shamans, and philosophical stoners who understood the mysteries of the universe.

During my travels I came to understand that we are all seeking truth and, in our own ways, finding it. I learnt from all these different people that the way to connect with the source of life is simple: have a heartfelt desire and commitment to do so, and the way will come to you. Unlike my upbringing, these conversations warmed my belly from the inside and offered a peace I had never experienced before.

As my world expanded, I found myself encountering the divine more often, first in dramatic ways, and then in more gentle and sustainable ways. One humid day during Thailand's rainy season, I was hiking on a narrow mountain path, and I slipped. As I was about to fall to my doom, a tree root sprung out of the ground and straddled my foot, steadying me until I regained my balance. Another time I was foolishly driving my motorbike home after a night out, going eighty kilometres an hour with a flat tyre (I don't endorse this behaviour). I hit a rock on the road and the bike started spinning out of control. I had that familiar thought again – *So, this is how I die* – before the motorbike suddenly righted itself and, magically, I found myself riding along safely in the right direction.

I know that being pulled out of a raging river, saved by a tree root and an autocorrecting motorbike might sound unbelievable to you. You may even wonder if all those years in the church made it difficult for me to distinguish between reality and fiction. But these stories are simply about trusting that life is made up of more than our rational mind can understand. You don't need to have had a near-death experience or to have grown up in a religious setting to believe that life can be mysterious. Perhaps for you this something 'more' is synchronicity, awe and wonder, or unconditional love.

You'll be pleased to know that over time, I began to live less recklessly and need saving less often. My connection to source began to feel more subtle, nuanced and accessible. Whenever I had lost my way and wasn't sure of my next life move, be it at work, in my love life or in my friendships, I would ask for guidance. And beautifully, I received it – sometimes accompanied by actual light shining into the room. When this happened, I would often remember the little girl in church using her whole mind, willing God to reveal itself to her, and I'd send her a loving smile.

After more than a decade of connecting to source, I became a wife, mother and business owner. At this time, I noticed that despite my spiritual steps forward, I was still carrying baggage from my past, namely, fear. I could feel a simmering resentment brewing towards the people that didn't give me the perfect childhood I imagined everyone else had enjoyed. I also had moments of rage that erupted from deep within my being and exploded out into the world when someone dared to, say, leave a wet towel on the floor. I didn't understand where the burning anger was coming from, but I knew it was an overreaction to the towel.

I dreamed of being a wise and jolly old woman, not a bitter, furious one. So, in my mid-thirties I set the intention of being healed by my fortieth birthday so I could enjoy inner freedom and joy in middle age. At the time, I had no idea how to heal from the past, but I trusted that I would find out. It didn't take long for the path to reveal itself: meditation. To my utter delight, meditation took me to all the places I didn't know I needed to go: the past, the future, outer space, my innermost world and into the present moment.

The biggest gift meditation gave me was creating a daily habit to pause, notice when I was caught in fear and intentionally move towards love. This may sound complicated or overly spiritual, but it's quite simple. For me, moving from fear to love meant that rather than accumulating new resentments that my future self would have to deal

During my travels I came to understand that we are all seeking truth and, in our own ways, finding it. I learnt from all these different people that the way to connect with the source of life is simple: have a heartfelt desire and commitment to do so, and the way will come to you.

with, I consciously faced difficulties as they arose and released them. Doing this practice once a day meant that when I turned forty, I no longer felt bitter or resentful about my past.

What I've learnt over the years is that fear is not limited to demons and horror, it can show up as snapping at loved ones when I feel misunderstood, feeling stressed waiting at a red light when I know I have time to spare or worrying so much about potentially getting cold that I stay home while everyone else goes swimming. Likewise, love is not all grand romantic gestures. It can present as a sense of peace during a difficult meeting, accepting a situation that can't be changed or a shift in mood that allows joy to enter.

First in meditation, then in everyday life, I've learnt how to observe my thoughts and emotions when they turn dark, as well as my fear-based reactions to life. I do this by feeling the sensations in my body – burning neck, quickened breath, for instance – allowing them all to be and pass on by. When my mind becomes still, I ask, *What would love look like right now?* The answer is usually simple and clear: *Be patient*, or, *Take a breath.* Suddenly, waiting at the red light becomes a welcome opportunity for stillness. From that peaceful state, I notice the spider showing off her freshly spun, geometrically perfect web, or the sunlight sparkling in the puddle at my feet, and that beautiful deep peace arrives.

My habit of moving from fear to love helps me in more challenging times too and shapes the way I respond to people. If I'm getting stressed because my son won't put on his shoes even though I've asked fourteen times, I notice my rising anger and pause to feel the sensations in my body. I resist the strong urge to shout and instead walk away and take a moment to let the anger pass through me. When I'm still, I ask quietly, *What would love look like now?* Then I remember that he's still a child and he doesn't have all the information. This understanding brings compassion for my son and my patience expands. Patience gives space for a new perspective to arise and suddenly the speed with which he puts on his shoes is so insignificant compared to the gratitude I have for his very existence. And usually, once I'm in this state of love, his shoes are already on, he's happily chatting away and we're out the door!

Nature helps me move from fear to love too. I was recently walking silently through an ancient forest, in awe of life manifested so intelligently and exquisitely, when I came across a rushing river. A flash of anxiety flooded my chest and the back of my neck as the memory of almost drowning struck my body. I felt the sensations and observed the fear in me. I noticed my thoughts about how dangerous rivers can be. And I practiced my habit. I asked the river, *What would love look like right now?* I heard: *You are not a thing that floats down the river; you are the river.*

I then imagined how it would feel to be the river, playfully rushing down the challenging rapids, then taking a rest to pool at the foot of a waterfall before flowing into the next exhilarating cascade. I was filled with joy as I imagined the river enjoying its own ride. And when I noticed my fear of drowning had moved into love, I laughed at how glorious life is when you seek the wisdom of the universe and hear its delicious replies.

I've realised that faith isn't about testing God or being saved, it's a gentle, long-term relationship with source. Whenever fear arises, I know that if I pay attention to what is here, right now, and I ask to be guided into love, my eyes will open to the beautiful aliveness that surrounds me, and I can access clarity, loving peace and joy. I can move from being swept along in the wild river begging to be saved, to becoming the river, flowing playfully through life.

Chapter Fourteen

The Healing Habits of a Highly Sensitive Person

American-born Sara Lynn Shemonsky was bright, successful ... and burnt-out. In therapy, she learnt three letters that unveiled a missing piece of clarity to the puzzle – and she remembered the beautiful and boundless healing power of the sunlight.

The clock hits 5pm, and as frequently happens at the end of another busy workday, I am physically, mentally and emotionally drained and depleted. I experience that familiar feeling of being both 'wired and tired' to the max. The intense sense of residual busyness buzzes like a powerful electrical current in my nervous system. The perpetual build-up of fatigue, tension and tightness feels like I'm carrying a heavy backpack full of boulders weighing down my shoulders. My mind races with replays and ruminations of the day's events, and my heart beats in overdrive from all the outpourings of emotional deposits of attention, gratitude and deep empathy I shared with others throughout the day.

As a full-time professional educator and part-time mindset coach in Loudoun County, Virginia, living and working amidst the constant hustling and bustling of the Washington DC metro area, I most often feel like this at the end of the day. It was all at its pinnacle when I was in my late twenties, when like so many in this stage of life, I was overly ambitious in striving to advance in my career. In those years gone by, I would constantly be giving every ounce of my energies outward and onward, running on caffeine and cortisol, aiming to 'prove' myself in my profession. I found it almost impossible to find healthy ways to naturally soothe myself and relax, especially at the end of the day. In fact, I would often beat myself up for feeling so 'on' all the time and ruminate in guilt for not being able to simply calm down and decompress after a busy day. My internal dialogue would press, *Why can't you navigate and cope with stress and overload as effectively as other people? Why do you feel as if the over-stimulations of the day impact you more deeply than others? Why can't you just shut it all off and settle down like your husband, family and friends all do?* Now, I know better, so I treat myself better.

I was thirty-four years old, in the spring of 2014, when a relapse of professional burnout sent me back to therapy, and I was introduced to a phrase that changed my life: Highly Sensitive Person (or HSP). The term, coined by psychologist Doctor Elaine Aron is used to describe a subset of the population with increased emotional and physical sensitivity, and heightened reactivity to daily internal and external stimuli, such as lights, noise, hunger and crowded spaces amongst other things. It's also referred to as sensory processing sensitivity (SPS), and I unequivocally have it. Over the years, I have learnt to own it and accept it. I have gained strategies to help navigate the world as an HSP.

Perhaps you can relate to my story and experience? Take a moment to reflect on the following questions, it could provide a helpful missing piece of your unique jigsaw puzzle.

- Are you easily overwhelmed by such things as bright lights, strong smells, coarse fabrics or loud sirens nearby?
- Do others' moods greatly impact you?
- Do you get rattled when you have a lot to do in a short amount of time?
- Do you make it a high priority to arrange your life to avoid upsetting or overwhelming situations?
- Do you have a rich and complex inner life?

These are just some of the questions Doctor Aron asks when a person suspects they might be highly sensitive. For me, it explained a lot – instantly. As Doctor Aron explains, this trait is not a new discovery, but it has been misunderstood. 'Because HSPs prefer to look before entering new situations, they are often called "shy",' she writes. 'But shyness is learned, not innate. In fact, 30% of HSPs are extroverts, although the trait is often mislabelled as introversion.' As much as I identify as an introvert, this statistic speaks volumes. As is human nature, all HSPs naturally crave and value deep connection; however, the daily challenges of constantly navigating the subtle and strong energies of the outside world greatly impact and vary in how we show up and 'present' ourselves to others.

When I discovered the term, I had a loving husband, a great group of friends and engaged in several joyful hobbies. My friends would have described me as loyal and fun-loving – so why did I often feel so depleted, overwhelmed, disconnected in my own body and even afraid – and how could I ease these feelings?

Through working with my therapist, I discovered that the burdens of my professional burnout were naturally connected to other demons lurking in my personal life. I was diagnosed with generalised anxiety disorder (GAD) and began to explore strategies to navigate the extreme 'pendulum swings' of perfectionism and people-pleasing that I felt daily.

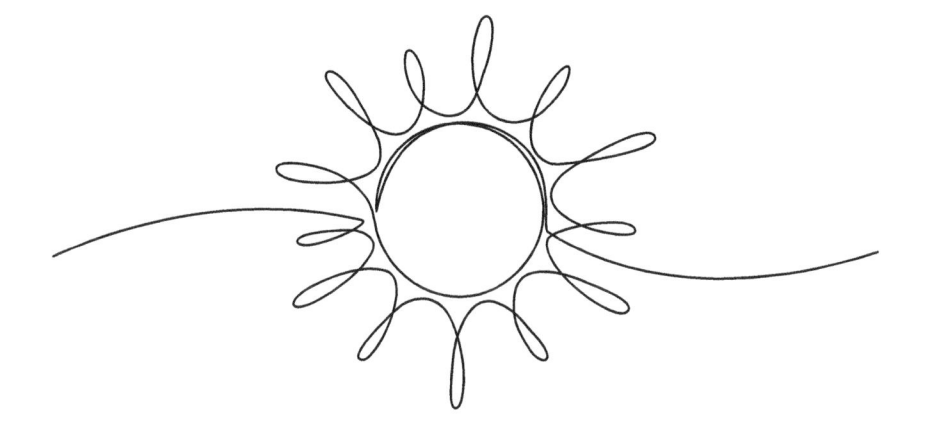

To help me better navigate and manage my personal reactivity to the outside world, I have begun to view my sensitivities not as a weakness or something to overcome, but as my own superpowers.

So, what soothing habits did I discover as a highly sensitive person navigating a highly stimulating world? I didn't discover a magical formula overnight, but now, ten years later, I have gained greater clarity and have shifted closer to an answer.

After this incident of burnout, I was lucky to find a local practice that offered a wide array of holistic, intuitive and alternative therapies, which sparked a pivotal moment in my own journey of healing. I found the power of meditation and breathwork to calm my dysregulated nervous system and soothe my highly sensitive tendencies' impact on my mind, heart and body. I was introduced to a wealth of self-compassion exercises that fostered a healing sense of acceptance within me. Plus, the mindful movements and flow of yoga allowed me to feel more attuned. I began to feel my body's chronic inflammation and autoimmune issues ease up and the flares starting to calm down.

It was through these years of hard work and 'heart work' that I came to realise that, at the core of all my striving and self-sabotage, was an innate desire to reconnect with my most-authentic self. I know, 'authenticity' can be a bit of a buzz phrase. To me, it simply meant living in alignment with my values and honouring a sense of 'coming home' to inner harmony. I was open to exploring healthier and more empowered ways to strengthen my inner world to better navigate the outer world with greater compassion and confidence.

Fast-forward to November 2023, and I discovered the magic ingredient for my healing habits. During a meditation workshop, a facilitator asked our group: 'When do you feel the most alive?' My mind's memory book opened, and a wave of vivid snapshots appeared, as if I was watching a movie about my favourite moments – a common colour palette, a familiar expression of joy on my face, a nostalgic feeling of freedom. There was a common thread in my most 'alive' memories – they all happened at sunrise or sunset. They also included movement and a chance to connect with nature. This was my answer as a forty-three-year-old woman, but I also instinctively knew these elements would be the same at any stage in my life. *This* is what made me feel the most alive.

I know what you may be thinking, *You can't spend your life chasing sunrises and sunsets.* Oh, but you can in a sense. I'm not saying you need to hike up a mountain every morning, but ever since I reflected on that question, I have paid attention to my activities during the precious 'golden hours', the period of daytime shortly after sunrise or before sunset. I realised that I have been doing this instinctively for my entire life, ever since I would relish the innocent delights of early autumn evenings growing up in north-eastern Ohio. There is something extra-special about this particular time of year in this particular place, when the summer daytime temperatures flirt with the impending cooler breezes ushering in at dusk. As an eight-year-old, I would climb a beautiful old oak tree outside our house at sunset – *my* climbing tree. I distinctly recall bringing my journal or my sketchpad with me on those evenings to write or draw as I perched in the branches. When I reflect on these memories, I am instantly transported back into a blissful state of vitality.

When I realised the importance of that trifecta – sunrises and sunsets, movement and spending time in nature – I began to view them as my 'anchors and arrows', the elements that most ground me and guide me back to my personal inner balance and harmony. What are the components of your anchors and arrows, those habits that act as an inner compass and feel like they bring you home to yourself? Take a moment to pause, think about what makes you feel the most alive and notice any patterns that emerge.

My anchors and arrows have continued to 'grow on and glow on' throughout the course of my life and no time do they shine brighter than when I am on summer holiday at the beach. My father, mother, older sister and I first visited the quaint resort town of Bethany Beach on the eastern shore of Delaware when I was just six years old. We all immediately fell in love with this charming seaside retreat, and it has remained my family's favourite vacation spot for four decades. Year in and year out, our beach trips epitomise the ultimate joyful summertime experience, celebrating rest, recalibration and reflection. To me, the early summer dusk by the ocean always offers the earth's most majestic masterpiece.

When I'm not on vacation, my anchor and arrow habits are more practical. I aim to find magical moments in the mundane, day-to-day doings. It could mean sitting outside in the warmth of early evening, nursing a favourite drink as the sun goes down, or it can be meeting a friend for an early morning walk at the pinnacle of a crisp daybreak. It may come from enjoying an energising daytime romp in the park with a beloved pet, or it could be felt by taking a freeing bike ride around town after work marvelling at the way the soft dusk highlights the skyline and cityscape.

Over the years, my anchors and arrows have guided me to greater inner wisdom, confidence and calm. But they haven't made me immune to the impact of being a highly sensitive person. To help me better navigate and manage my personal reactivity to the outside world, I have begun to view my sensitivities not as a weakness or something to overcome, but as my own superpowers. Over the last few years, I've created a practice that incorporates the healing power of my trifecta habits, I call it GLIMMER. I'm not going to lie, it might *sound* like a lot to do; however, by setting aside fifteen to thirty minutes on a regular basis, this practice has become an incredible remedy for my highly sensitive nervous system and something that helps me to show up for the work that I really enjoy, without feeling frazzled at 5pm.

G: Gazing at the sky, the sunset and tuning into the natural beauty of the season.

L: Leaning in and listening to my body, mind and heart in the moment.

I: Intentional inhales (breathwork).

M: Movement (yoga flow).

M: Meditation.

E: Expansive exhales (breathwork).

R: Reflection.

Here is a taste of a typical GLIMMER routine experience. I open my front door and step out onto our wooden front porch. I immediately feel a cool and refreshing spring breeze sweep across my face and I can smell the damp earthy sweetness of fresh spring grass emerging after winter's frozen spell. First, I focus my attention and awareness on the sunset's glow, and I begin to connect with my body and breath. I lean in and listen to my body for any signs or signals of pain or discomfort, as well as what may be swirling in my mind or heavy in my heart. I take a long inhale, pause at the top and encourage one more sip of air in. I hold my breath for a moment before releasing with a strong exhale and soft sigh. I do this for three rounds or more.

Next, I lay out my yoga mat and do several sun salutations. I visualise the sunset as an altar and my sun salutations as sacred offerings. When my body feels a bit looser and calmer, I find a seat, either on a chair or on my mat, and settle in for a guided meditation. I choose a topic or theme that seems to resonate with the energies of my day, and what I may need in the moment to empty my tank. The end of meditation always serves as an open-door invitation for reflection. Most often, I find that writing in my journal is my ultimate form of creative expression.

My GLIMMER routine has been instrumental in helping me

As I reflect on my personal journey, look back on my childhood and see that innocent eight-year-old climbing my favourite old oak tree, I have great admiration and appreciation for my younger self. How wonderful that I instinctively knew how to soothe my nervous system by seeking out and relishing in the awe, wonder and pure power of the sunlight.

decompress at the end of the day. It feels like making a physical, emotional and mental 'deposit' to balance out all the 'withdrawals' I've made throughout the day as I move through the world as a highly sensitive person. The quality of my sleep has improved. My moods throughout the day feel more balanced. I feel less triggered and reactionary. I am less thrown about my other people's experiences. I have stronger boundaries at work. Absolutely, there are nights when I don't want to do it or I am feeling extra pressed with time, but I acknowledge the resistance and do it anyway. It's a big commitment but, to me, it is worth it.

Today, I live more joyfully with my beloved husband, Brian, and our two rescue dogs, Pippa and Poe. I am honest with my husband about elements of day-to-day life that make me feel overwhelmed and overstimulated. He now recognises my highly sensitive tendencies and triggers and respects the importance of my evening GLIMMER routine for myself and our relationship. After enjoying my trifecta, I re-enter my home and life more able to offer my relationship the loving attention it deserves.

As I reflect on my personal journey, look back on my childhood and see that innocent eight-year-old climbing my favourite old oak tree, I have great admiration and appreciation for my younger self. How wonderful that I instinctively knew how to soothe my nervous system by seeking out and relishing in the awe, wonder and pure power of the sunlight. I began life following my inner compass and now, I've returned to what was always there, a deep belief that I know what I need and how to soothe myself. That's my greatest advice for adults, whether highly sensitive or not. Get to know your own personal anchors and arrows and honour them. May you all continue to 'Grow on and glow on!'

Chapter Fifteen

You Are Beautiful

Life coach Margie Dannenbaum lived at the mercy of her inner critic. Then, one day, a stranger handed her daughter a sticker – and it sent the mother of four on a new pathway to healing.

Four years ago, my daughter was working at our local ice cream shop when a customer's actions had a ripple effect, first impacting my daughter and then, as an after-effect, me.

Marlee, my daughter, was twenty-two years old at the time and had been working at The Dairy Bar in Margate, New Jersey, between graduating college and going to graduate school. Whilst Margate was a sleepy beach town for most of the year, the lines for ice cream were always long and colourful on the weekends over summer. Everyone would flock to this iconic place known for its old-fashioned architecture, teal and pink exterior and delicious sweet treats.

Marlee was coming up to the end of her shift when an outgoing woman with beautiful grey hair came to the window and handed her a shiny silver sticker. It read: *You Are Beautiful*. I remember my daughter coming home from work, all tired and sticky from scooping ice cream, and excitedly showing me the sticker and sharing the story. She said, 'Look what Rachel from Chicago gave me.' Her joy was palpable. I saw how this one simple gesture made her night.

Straightaway, I decided to order some of these stickers to give out myself. I loved the idea of spreading this message and it reminded me of something I had done during the COVID-19 pandemic a year earlier.

During my long recovery from COVID-19, I made beaded chains that could be attached to a mask. I made so many that I began giving them out to my friends. I took this one step further by putting the chains inside a little mesh bag with a card that said 'kindness matters'. I gave out over 250 of these little bags to strangers. Doing this brought me joy at a difficult time in my life.

I loved the feeling of surprising someone with an act of kindness. I knew firsthand how one gesture could make a difference in a person's day. Since the days of mask-wearing were over, the *You Are Beautiful* stickers seemed like a wonderful alternative for me.

Whilst I couldn't articulate it clearly at the time, part of me was wanting to help others find something in themselves that I was yearning for myself: self-love. You see, for as long as I could remember, my inner critic ruled my thoughts and ultimately my life. It was so strong I even gave her a name, 'Cage'.

Like so many women today, I grew up surrounded by misogynistic beliefs that over time, I took on as my own. I learnt from an early age that it was my responsibility to make sure the needs of those around me were met before my own. I lived in service to others, not my own inner knowing. I relied on the actions of others to make me feel worthy.

My thoughts were consumed by 'if, then' scenarios. *If* I lose the weight, *then* I will feel better. *If* he empties the dishwasher, *then* he really loves me. *If* she 'listens', *then* I will be validated. I believed I would feel better if others changed and when they did not change or listen to me it was because there was something wrong with me.

Despite this inner monologue, I managed to create a beautiful and well-rounded life. As I write this, I am happily married, have four wonderful adult children and fulfilling friendships. I hold two master's degrees, have held significant leadership roles in my community and enjoyed a successful and rewarding career. But, despite all this outward achievement and success, for many years, on the inside, I felt like I was broken and not enough.

'Cage', my inner critic, became even louder after contracting COVID-19 and becoming a 'covid long hauler'. I was experiencing neuropathy in my arms and legs, brain fog and full-body weakness. I developed a new autoimmune disease, linear morphea, that was shrinking the ligaments in my ankle. Simple things I used to take for granted like wearing shoes became difficult. I was a physical mess. 'Cage' noticed my vulnerability and seized the moment to speak to me even more strongly.

This time, she directed her attention outwards, I was judging others and the circumstances of my life harshly. I became mad at the world and the people around me. My thoughts had me convinced that all my suffering was caused by other people's behaviours and actions or non-actions. I was unsatisfied, irritable and afraid. I believed everything was happening to me because I was broken. Something had to change. I yearned to be free from my inner critic. Yet, I was terrified to ask for help. Perhaps you can remember a time when you felt this uncomfortable combination of emotions too?

I finally reached out to a therapist friend who suggested I join her Mastering Your Mind program to learn how to stop sabotaging joy and happiness and find self-expression and inner confidence.

When I said yes to this program (and to myself), I was in the early stages of giving out the You Are Beautiful stickers. At this point, I loved giving out the stickers, but Cage was still loud, and I did not feel beautiful myself. Witnessing someone receive this message did warm my heart, but not enough to make me believe that I was beautiful too.

When I first began to give out the stickers it felt awkward. What should I say? How do I decide who to give a sticker to? Only women? Will my gesture make someone else uncomfortable? But of course, the most burning question was: Am I qualified to give these stickers out when I don't myself believe that I am beautiful? Am I an imposter? But despite this inner rumbling, I continued to give out the stickers. I trusted in the process. Something was stirring deep inside of me. Could it be self-love?

The reactions I receive when I hand someone a sticker are varied. Sometimes, people hug me. Sometimes, people are shy. Often people get teary. People often bring their hands to their chest and give me an 'ohhhh that is so nice'. Some people are suspicious: am I trying to sell them something? I've observed, firsthand, how bad we can be at accepting compliments and trusting the intentions of the people who want to connect with us. Regardless of the varied responses, each time I witnessed a smile and a shoulder drop. Time and time again.

As I write this, I have given out over 4,500 stickers to friends and strangers alike. I often see the stickers places I go in my community. At the cash register where I get my haircut. On the back of people's phones. On the waitresses' billfold at my favourite restaurant. Seeing the stickers brings me so much joy. I feel a little lighter each time.

One moment when the impact of giving out the stickers became clear to me was when I was having a hard day. My mother-in-law, who I have known my whole life, was not doing well. I had recently learned about my sixty-five-year-old brother's early Alzheimer's diagnosis. And my dad's health was beginning to fail. We had recently moved this proud, accomplished man to a nursing home because he was no longer able to care for himself. I felt sad and alone, so I decided to go for a little retail therapy. Although I knew it wouldn't create true happiness, I hoped a little dopamine hit would feel good, if only for a moment.

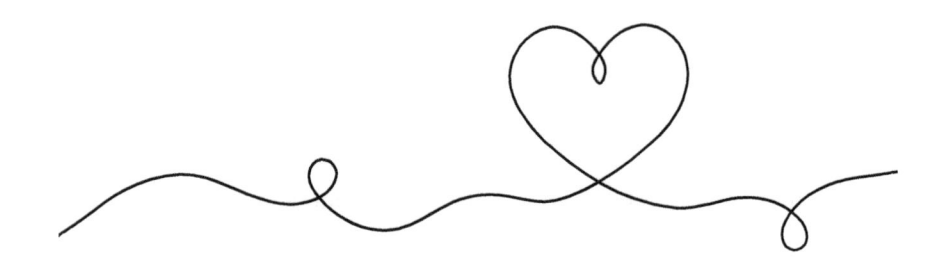

As I write this, I have given out over 4,500 stickers to friends and strangers alike. I often see the stickers places I go in my community. At the cash register where I get my haircut. On the back of people's phones. On the waitresses' billfold at my favourite restaurant. Seeing the stickers brings me so much joy. I feel a little lighter each time.

As I was browsing in Lululemon, a woman who worked there approached me. She wanted to know if I was the person who gave her the sticker a few weeks earlier. I said yes. She then shared with me how receiving that message, at that moment, had a positive impact in her life. She wanted to thank me. She had tears in her eyes. She asked me if she could give me a hug. I cried too. At that moment, I felt the true impact of one small gesture.

Giving out the stickers has given me a tangible way to express gratitude for people around me and for my life. It has helped me to experience joy in a whole new way. My relationships are stronger. My thoughts about my life are more colourful. I have found my own, unique voice. Each time I watch others receive the message 'You Are Beautiful', I can see my own light more clearly. It didn't happen overnight, but somewhere along the way, I learnt to see my own beauty. What a gift it is, for them and for me.

Yes, I still experience the dark and hard parts of what it means to be a human, however, I connect to the light that lives inside of me and truly see that I am not broken. Seeing such a dramatic change occur from a simple daily habit was proof that, even those limiting beliefs you think are permanent can be challenged – and it might happen in the most unlikely ways.

Breaking free from 'Cage' has helped me so much. I have unhooked from the idea that my weight has anything to do with my worth. I have built new friendships that fill me with joy. I have carved out a new career path as a life coach helping other people to challenge their inner monologue.

As I was halfway through writing this chapter, my father passed away. The pain is still acute as I write these words, but my experience is very different from when my mother passed away six and a half years ago. When my mother passed, I was sad, but I focused on gratitude. After all, I had a mother who instilled so many wonderful qualities inside of me. I avoided truly feeling my grief because I had to be strong for my dad and the rest of our family. So, I soldiered on.

Looking back, I can see hiding behind gratitude was a theme for me. I did not think that I deserved to be sad because my life was filled with privilege and security. After recovering from COVID-19, I felt similarly. I was so filled with gratitude that I did not die that I didn't process the trauma and the fear that I felt when I was so sick. Like many people – especially women – I thought it would seem ungrateful to grieve and show fear and, so, I pushed those feelings down. What's worse, I believed that, if I showed my grief, the world would see how broken I truly was.

Now, thanks to nearly four years of the sticker project and learning to challenge my limiting beliefs, I can understand that everyone deserves to feel their emotions – especially emotions as natural and understandable as grieving and sadness. So, with my dad's death, I am taking the time to sit in my pain. It hurts as it passes through me, and I am okay. I am sad, but I am not suffering. It will take me time to process all that I feel losing my dad, but I have the tools to grieve in a whole new way. And who knows, maybe I will be able to grieve my mom in a deeper way now too.

For the first time in my life, I am truly living and understanding my life according to me. It's easy to get caught up in reading books or taking courses on living authentically without taking action. A huge part of my journey has been about small intentional actions that gain momentum over time. Giving out the stickers is just one example. I have also adopted a meditation and journalling practice. I continue to nourish my body with foods that allow me to feel my best. I ask for help or a hug when I need it. I challenge Cage, my inner critic, daily. I exercise. I listen deeply to those around me. All these simple habits are having a powerful impact.

There is something about moving through the world telling people

There is something about moving through the world telling people they are beautiful that makes it impossible not to send yourself the same love and compassion.

they are beautiful that makes it impossible not to send yourself the same love and compassion. I wonder if there is something in your life that allows you to feel kindness towards yourself or others? For you, it may be a gentle wind-down ritual at the end of a busy day. It could be volunteering or prepping an extra dinner for your elderly neighbour. Or would choosing not to spread gossip, or telling a mother who is struggling with their toddler in the supermarket that they're doing brilliantly feel like an intentional action for you? Life can be hard for everyone. We can all help each other get through, and every positive habit shines back at you.

Sometimes, I think of all the people I've given stickers to – an army of 4,500 people – and I hope they were inspired to pass on that compliment or to offer someone else a little care or compassion. Now, when I give out the stickers, I give the person several. I ask them, if they are comfortable, to please give at least one of them to a stranger. Paying it forward creates a ripple that I love being a part of.

I did recently hear that a young woman I gave some stickers to brought them to an inner-city dance program where she volunteers. She gave them to all the young students. This is not the only story like this. I know of several people who have ordered the stickers and are now giving them out themselves. Wow!

I don't think one sticker has the power to change someone's life, but it could ignite a spark. I understand I am not responsible, nor am I able, to make someone else happy. We are the only ones who can decide how we feel about ourselves. I choose, however, to offer simple yet powerful acts of kindness to both myself and others and trust that it is making a difference.

Remember, you are beautiful.

Chapter Sixteen

From Acorn to Oak

As a child growing up in Midwest America, Tom Macior escaped into nature whenever possible. It would take over fifty years to truly uncover what he was escaping from – just in time to embrace the best years of his life.

It started with a gentle breeze and grew into a raging storm. Giant, billowing clouds rolled in – greenish-grey, purplish hues giving way to blackened silhouettes flashing a promise of an awe-inspiring show from above. I was seven or eight years old at the time, playing baseball with friends at the sanctuary we escaped to from our family ills – a local park that contained a magnificent wood of century-old white oak trees.

The first flash of lightning illuminated the sky, an ominous warning that sent my friends and me scrambling home on our bikes as fast as our gangly legs could pedal. I arrived just as the first pellets of rain fell from the menacing skies and ran to my bedroom to watch the fury from the same window perch where I often looked outside longingly, after experiencing dysfunctional forms of discipline that I was taught I somehow deserved. In that moment, I looked outside with a new perspective. No longer was I looking out in pain, I was firmly engaged in the moment. The storm brought wave after wave of lightning and thunder, filling my soul with a sense of awe and wonder. While slightly scary, the powerful force of the storm was inspiring. It awakened my soul to see that there is something much bigger out there than I imagined.

White pellets hailed from the sky, bounced off the ground and collected across the yard into pools of magical white pearls. And then, as quickly as it started, it ended. The wind ceased, the clouds parted and streaks of warm, loving sunshine pierced the dark sky as if heaven itself was appearing before me. Through the window, rays of light fell upon my face and filled me with warmth, a peaceful calm and silence replaced the violent forces I had witnessed just moments ago. As the storm dramatically ended, birds began to sing a beautiful cheerful song that seemed to be celebrating life, or perhaps, just happily expressing their deliverance from the storm. Ironically, it was Good Friday and the storm occurred late in the afternoon, similar to the time of day and weather conditions that I was taught happened during the crucifixion and passing of Christ. Soaking this in felt peaceful and connected me to something bigger than myself, replacing the loneliness I often experienced with my family.

Fifty years later, I can better understand the gift that was introduced to me on that day. Nature connected me with the here and now, it offered solace and serenity, a place to escape, surrender and feel happy, connected and present. Whenever I was in nature, my attention was focused on experiencing the moment. Instead of being at home and 'reading the tea leaves' for signs of danger – a look, a mood, a comment – I could escape to my natural world and feel at ease. From the age of seven or eight, I spent as much time outdoors as my school days would allow. At the time, the suburbs of Chicago still offered plenty of creeks, ponds, woods and prairies to discover. Each environment provided unique opportunities to investigate and explore – tadpoles that turned into frogs, furry caterpillars that turned into butterflies, fireflies that enhanced the night sky with their magical flickering glow and earthworms that were both male and female – anything in nature seemed possible. That observation created hope, perhaps I could dream of a better future for myself?

The more time I spent in nature's embrace, the more I began to experience a deeper connectedness with something that felt divine. Curiosity led me to discover my inner light well before I was introduced to meditation. Sitting outside in my favourite hideouts, I would often close my eyes, hoping to reconnect with the uplifting light energy that I had often experienced between my eyes. At the time, all I knew is that it made me feel safe, peaceful and happy.

I began to feel an appreciation for even the simplest acts of nature that filled me with joy. Each autumn, I relished walking through the majestic white oak woods by my home, stretching my arms around their century-old trunks and observing their acorns as they fell from the sky wearing their fuzzy little frond hats. *Thud, thud, thud, WHOOPS, crunch, crunch!* Even in my missteps I could feel safe as the squirrels seemed to appreciate the benefits of my clumsiness.

Nature also offered me opportunities to navigate my feelings in a healthy manner, which was a challenging endeavour at home. When a small bulldozer appeared in our yard and removed the bushes and green sanctuary of my pretend hideaways and forts, I was deeply saddened. Watching the maple tree I grew up with being cut down was painful. However, that opportunity taught me that I could feel sad without having to hold onto the pain. In my sorrow I came up with the idea of honouring my friend by taking a section of the saw man's cutting and making a drinking cup out of it. Even though my nascent wood-carving skills were ill-equipped for the task, my heart took pleasure in trying to stay connected to the sapling that I grew up with. In the end,

Each environment provided unique opportunities to investigate and explore – tadpoles that turned into frogs, fireflies that enhanced the night sky with their magical flickering glow and earthworms that were both male and female – anything in nature seemed possible. That observation created hope, perhaps I could dream of a better future for myself?

I settled on closing my eyes and envisioned myself standing beside my friend, thanking it for the cool shade it provided in the summer, the strong branches that offered me a bird's-eye view of the world and the wonderful hues of reddish gold leaves it painted and gently released to the ground each fall, creating billowy piles and another playground for my imagination.

Another experience taught me about courage and the importance of following my moral compass while witnessing how some human beings treated nature. On one of those autumn days in the white oak woods, I came across a group of older boys that appeared to be making a fire inside a trash can. As I walked near them, they laughed and asked if I wanted to see what they were doing. To my horror, I looked into the bin and saw that they had captured and were seeking to harm a woodland creature. Reacting without thinking, I pushed over the can and ran away as fast as I could. I looked back to happily see the chipmunk escape back into its burrow. Witnessing such cruelty has forever changed me, leaving little tolerance for bullies, injustice or those unkind.

Growing up in the sixties often felt frightening and chaotic. Nature became my retreat, offering solace and serenity as well as providing life lessons that have shaped my core values and beliefs. And most of all it offered a safe place to experience the innocence and joy of simply being a child.

I wish I could end my story here, but life is constantly changing. While I have always maintained a close relationship with our natural world, the choices I made pulled me in different directions. Now, looking back, I see that my relationship with nature has evolved, reflecting the twists and turns of my own journey along the way. During my teens, nature provided a different type of escape, a place to go camping with friends and party far away from the judgemental eyes of parents. While fun, these experiences began the path of dulling my senses. Later as a young adult, nature offered a welcoming respite from the challenges of career and the confinements of urban living, however, for a while, I fell into the mindset that faster was better. It was all about how I could push my own limits, which led me to lose touch with the healing power of nature.

From my thirties to fifties, my journey began to follow a different path as career and financial success absorbed most of my energy. Control was the driving force behind my endeavours and the more I committed to this path, the more spiritually lost I felt. Even when I ventured for a walk in the woods, my mind was thinking about my career or the financial trappings of the physical world. I soon found myself being pulled further away from being present and experiencing divine connection; I started to ignore my inner compass and made choices that led me astray. That lonely feeling returned, and I aimlessly tried to fill the void by choosing partners, experiences and things that failed to bring me happiness. At times my life felt rudderless and empty. Thankfully, nature and the divine are a mystical force that presented me with many small miracles that caught my attention and helped guide me through some of my darkest days. At times it was something simple and at other times, more profound such as the experience I had during the honeymoon of my second marriage.

It was autumn in Costa Rica and the rainy season lived up to its name, weather conditions had been extremely stormy and dreary for over a week. Several events occurred that were as painful as my first 'newlywed experience', eliciting feelings of fear and despair. At the end of the trip while driving back over the continental divide, I looked in the rearview mirror and saw that the dark storm clouds had finally begun to part, exposing glorious rays of sunshine that reminded me of my boyhood experience over thirty years ago. In that very moment, a gentle voice spoke within: *You are never alone, I am always here with you.* That voice, vision and connection has stayed with me and has offered hope and guidance through some difficult times. Ten years later, when the marriage ended, I reflected on that moment and the salvation that nature consistently offered me throughout my life.

The relationship did however produce a miracle in the birth of my daughter, Olivia, who reignited my passion for our natural world. After forty years of 'worldly experiences' I naively believed that I was ready to participate in the important task of raising a child. Unfortunately, as a first-time father, the 'how to' books I read often missed the mark and failed to provide the type of advice I needed most. Given the travel demands of my job, I tried to spend as much time as possible with Olivia whenever I was home. It was during one of my flailing attempts of child care that I stumbled back into the healing arms of nature. One night, when we were on a family holiday and nothing would soothe our colicky baby, desperation led me to take Olivia for a stroll on the beach at 4am. The sound of the ocean waves were soothing, the sun coming up over the horizon was heavenly and the dolphins that suddenly appeared offshore were magical. Olivia calmed down and was cooing, soothed as me by simple acts of nature. From that moment forward, we spent most of our time together outdoors exploring all that mother nature had to offer. Strapping Liv to my chest for a walk in the woods or biking with her along the Potomac River in her little child seat was the norm.

As she grew up, I treasured seeing the joy she expressed while exploring our natural world. I relished seeing her delightful expressions while sniffing the sweet fragrance of wildflowers, her keen awareness while listening to songbirds in a meadow or seeing her little footprints disappear in the surf as she excitedly gathered 'sea glass jewels' and discovered new tidal pool creatures. Even rainy days became fun days as she beckoned me to join her outside for a tea party under my giant golf umbrella or to follow her lead as she merrily splashed in puddles in her matching duckie boots and umbrella. The innocence and appreciation

Growing up in the sixties often felt frightening and chaotic. Nature became my retreat, offering solace and serenity as well as providing life lessons that have shaped my core values and beliefs. And most of all it offered a safe place to experience the innocence and joy of simply being a child.

she expressed filled me with joy and reconnected me with my habit and friend.

While the joys of fatherhood provided happiness and balance, it was only a matter of time before interpersonal challenges and my career swayed me back into 'the void'. For most of my life, I have avoided the pain required to heal and truly evolve, often leading me to make decisions that did not serve my soul's best interest. I've also discovered that, while my determination and drive has provided professional and financial rewards, it has come at a steep price. Life lessons for me have not been learned quickly, repeating my survival patterns and begrudgingly learning through the 'school of hard knocks'. With profound gratitude, I am here to share that it is never too late to change! I've come to learn that, by surrendering and being curious, one can earnestly learn from their past, evolve and reclaim their highest self. In my journey, understanding and accepting self-love is the core.

The truth is, I originally pushed back on participating in this book as work kept me 'much too busy' to find the time. And then, as life would have it, a few weeks later I was suddenly released by my employer – and I had the freedom to participate. First, I needed to do some deep soul searching. It was hard to admit that, after thirty-seven years, I was exhausted and done; yet I was also concerned about losing my identity and sense of purpose. With the help of mentors and professionals, I finally began to look at the patterns and pain that have usurped me throughout my life. During one session with my mentor, the topic of shame came up. Shame? I resented the word and its implications to my sense of self. I chose to protect myself and pushed back, strongly proclaiming, 'I've done my work, I'm not sure I have anything to feel shamed about!' And, as far as self-love goes, 'Of course I love myself, I believe I'm a good person.' My mentor quietly listened and compassionately asked, 'Well, then, do you feel you are lovable?' *Ughh,* ouch! The question burst my defensive bubble and unfurled a deep isolated pain that I've kept deeply buried throughout my life – a sense of loneliness that nature has eased but never completely erased.

That moment taught me that as much as I've tried, there are no magical cures, drugs, partners or experiences that can fill the void if we do not understand and love ourselves. Thankfully, nature has been a patient guide in nudging me along the way. I'm slowly relearning that, by being present and surrendering to the divine, it is possible to heal pain by loving oneself. The lessons and work are endless, but the rewards are great. And, oddly, it seems that the more I lean into surrendering, the easier life gets. After sixty-two years on this earth, I have solemnly begun the process of healing and reclaiming the spirit and appreciation for life that I had as a child.

I now live on a barrier island off the South Carolina coast and am grateful to awaken each day and experience a diverse variety of wildlife that captures my attention, appreciation and wonder: pelicans, sea turtles, herons, ospreys, egrets, hummingbirds, bobcats, deer and alligators abound. A small, rare bird called the red knot migrates over nine thousand miles from Patagonia to the Artic Circle and makes its lone stop here on their journey to feed and rest. Local dolphins have taught themselves to 'strand feed', a method of schooling fish onto the shoreline and then beaching themselves temporarily to feast. The local islands here are one of the few places in the entire world where these events can be observed. I spend hours each day, walking, biking, observing and soaking it all in. And in the summer, as the heat and humidity reach a crescendo in the late afternoon sky, magnificent towering storm clouds appear that connect me to my youth and once again humble me as I watch one of nature's greatest shows.

As I enter the best years of my life, with a loving, supportive partner, and family and friends all around me, nature brings me heartfelt gratitude, without needing to be an escape from my pain. I am looking forward to embracing retirement and continuing my growth from acorn to oak.

Chapter Seventeen

Finding Strength in Words

As a single mother in Vietnam, Tang Duyen Hong faced significant cultural and social stigma that amplified the challenges she faced. Hong had two choices: to accept the fact that her life would be lonely and full of barriers, or to use her voice to empower other women. She chose the latter, and her daily habit became a movement.

I grew up in one of the many quiet coastal villages of central Vietnam. I remember those long summer months when the heat was oppressive and relentless. Even the wind whispering through the Annamite Mountains carried a stifling heat. For hours each day, all you could hear was the chorus of cicadas.

I also grew up in the aftermath of the American War. My father journeyed to Europe in search of education and opportunity. My mother was left to provide for our family. When I was eleven years old, my mother made the heart-wrenching decision to leave me behind as she went searching for work. Like many women, she felt like she didn't have a choice.

I was left under the care of my grandfather. My grandmother had just died, and everyone thought it was best that I stay there. Even though I only weighed 30kg, when I wasn't at school, I was tasked with managing the household chores. I cooked, cleaned and tended to the sprawling garden that seemed to stretch endlessly into the horizon. I also took care of my younger cousins, one who had lost both parents. The echoes of the war lingered in the air. Poverty, scarcity, grief, loss and conflict seeped into every aspect of life in the coastal village I called home.

As I grew older, I became acutely aware of the disparities within my family. My father, with his European education and unfamiliarity with the realities of war-torn Vietnam, struggled to comprehend the hardships faced by my mother and her generation. Meanwhile, my mother, with her stoic resilience and unwavering determination, carried the weight of her past with her; a constant reminder of the trials she had endured and continued to endure.

As a teenager, I struggled to navigate the divide in my family and to reconcile the complexities of our history. I felt alone and like my voice or experience didn't matter. In my attempts to bridge this gap, I often found myself caught between two worlds, unable to fully belong to either. And this is how I found my way to the healing habit of writing. Every night during my adolescence, I poured out my heart and soul onto the blank canvas before me. I was young, but I already had a lot to say. I can still remember huddling in the corner of my makeshift bedroom with only a candle to shine a light on my journal.

In those moments of solitude, the words became my refuge; a silent witness to the turmoil raging within me. I wrote about my dream of living in a complete family with a mum and a dad, shared meals and time for play. I wrote about my aspirations of achieving something big and perhaps travelling the world one day, just like my father.

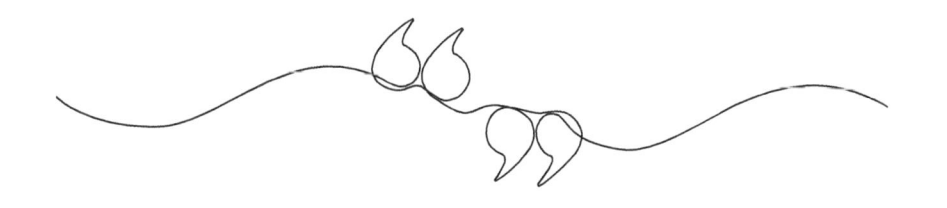

As a teenager, I struggled to navigate the divide in my family and to reconcile the complexities of our history. I felt alone and like my voice or experience didn't matter. In my attempts to bridge this gap, I often found myself caught between two worlds, unable to fully belong to either. And this is how I found my way to the healing habit of writing.

As well as writing, I became a passionate reader. Thanks to our village library, I devoured books with a hunger bordering on obsession, losing myself in the worlds of distant lands and star-crossed lovers. In the pages of books, I found a sense of belonging that had long eluded me. Here I was free to lose myself in my imagination and the weight of my burdens lifted, even if it was just for a moment.

The library keeper, perhaps out of necessity rather than kindness, entrusted me with the keys to the library, allowing me to roam freely amidst the rows of dusty books and weathered newspapers. What a gift that was for me. With no-one else to claim the space, the library became my sanctuary. From the sweeping epics of *Gone with the Wind* to the tumultuous saga of *The Thorn Birds*, I allowed myself to get lost in the worlds of other people.

In the eyes of the villagers, I was a solitary figure. As I retreated into books, I felt even more isolated and different from the other children in the village. Unable to relate to their simple joys and mundane concerns, I withdrew further into myself. Driven by a fierce determination to impress my 'worldly' father, I threw myself into my studies with unwavering focus and dedication. At school, I received multiple awards for my writing. While my name was proudly shared by my uncles, aunts and grandfather with the villagers, no-one took the time to read my words. It didn't matter. I kept on writing.

I had no idea that over fifteen years later, writing would become my sanctuary and a lifeline when I felt cast out by the country that I called home.

Raised on a diet of romanticised fiction and isolated from the realities of human connection, I was ill-equipped to navigate the complexities of adult relationships and responsibilities. Just two days after parting ways with my boyfriend, I found myself staring at two pink lines on a pregnancy test that would forever alter the trajectory of my life. Single. Pregnant. Twenty-six years old.

In that pivotal moment, a whirlwind of emotions swept through me – joy, confusion, sadness, loneliness and apprehension. As the reality of my situation sank in, I was faced with a choice between fear and courage – uncertainty and determination. At the time, I was living with my brother. I had a respectable job in a non-government organisation, earning a good salary. I was a capable woman who could look after herself. The most challenging part of it was the stigma and gossip surrounding my situation. It made me stressed and lonely. As soon as I was visibly pregnant, I heard the whispers of disapproval and judgement. I felt like an outcast in a world that prized conformity.

In Vietnam, the number of households headed by single mothers has grown significantly in the last three decades; however, stigma, disadvantage and income instability can make life difficult for these women. There is no financial support from the government and no mandatory structures for fathers to pay child support. Adding to the social and financial challenges these women face is also the fact that many of them have been in unhealthy relationships and experienced domestic violence.

When I was about six months pregnant, one of my close friends lost her child due to a disease. I tried to support her emotionally, but she and her family refused to acknowledge the loss. They acted as if nothing had happened, believing that since she had lost an eight-month-old baby, she could simply have another. She was forced to ignore her feelings and move on. During this time, I was also receiving hurtful comments from some of my female colleagues. Some of them even suggested that I had trapped the father of my baby by getting pregnant. These experiences led me to dream about a better community and society – one where women uplift and support each other. So, I started to create this world through my words.

I'll never forget pressing 'publish' on my first blog post – an introduction into who I was and the future I was hoping to create. I was nervous and apprehensive but I never doubted the impact of this blog. On some level, I knew it was going to be important.

The blog became more than just a platform for self-expression; it became a lifeline and a beacon of hope in a world that often seemed dark and unforgiving. Through the power of writing, I found the strength to rise above the whispers of doubt and condemnation. Each word became a testament to my unwavering resolve, a declaration of defiance in the face of adversity.

As I shared my story with the world and my experience of being a single mother in Vietnam, I found that I was not alone. Other women from all walks of life and backgrounds reached out to me, sharing their own struggles and triumphs in the journey of single motherhood. Their stories, like mine, were marked by hardship and heartache, yet tinged with a resilience and strength that defied all odds.

Over fifteen years, my community grew to 210,000 subscribers, and I was responsible for the largest online community of single mothers in Vietnam. Through my words, I had created a community of kindred spirits who no longer wanted to be silenced. Together we formed a sisterhood.

Driven by a new-found sense of purpose, I embarked on a mission to make a difference in the lives of single mothers everywhere. Thus, Catalyst for Change was born – an organisation dedicated to empowering single mothers through community education and support.

At the heart of our organisation is an online community where single mothers can come together to share their stories, find support and forge meaningful connections. Through our platform, we offer a range of resources and services, from vocational training and psychotherapy to business support and mentorship.

Every day brings new challenges and obstacles, but I remain steadfast in my commitment to making a difference. For with each life we touch, each woman we empower, we were not just changing the trajectory of her life – we were building a better future for generations to come.

As I reflect on the journey that has led me to this moment, I am struck by the profound impact that writing has had on my life. What began as a solitary pursuit in my childhood bedroom transformed into a means of navigating the complexities of my own existence as a young adult. And then over time, it blossomed into a powerful force for change, shaping not only my own destiny but the lives of countless others.

Perhaps as you read this, you are reflecting on a hobby or habit of yours that has changed over time too? Is there something in your life that began as a way to escape or manage your inner turmoil and turned into something that provides greater meaning and connection?

For nearly fifteen years, I have walked this path of self-discovery. I have shared my stories and amplified the voices of those whose struggles too often go unheard. Along the way, I have been met with words of admiration and praise – 'How strong you are,' they say – but I've also been met with criticism. Colleagues have said I am too open about my experiences. Others have commented on how speaking about my life as a single mother brings shame to my ex's family. Some of my other friends, including high school friends, are afraid I might have an affair with their husbands. But I believe this is how we know we're doing something important. When we make the invisible visible, when we challenge the stereotypes, the stigma and the shame, it will make some people uncomfortable, and that's okay.

Today, I run the largest support group for single mothers in Vietnam, enabling women to be free from stigma, abuse and shame. Our work includes offering free counselling and vocational training, family planning support, and English classes for the children of single mothers. We also provide small loans to single women who are interested in starting a small business.

As I reflect on the journey that has led me to this moment, I am struck by the profound impact that writing has had on my life. What began as a solitary pursuit in my childhood bedroom transformed into a means of navigating the complexities of my own existence as a young adult. And then over time, it blossomed into a powerful force for change, shaping not only my own destiny but the lives of countless others.

It was through the act of writing that I found the courage to reconcile my past and forge a new path forward. Today, I am committed to amplifying the voices of other single mothers in my community, shining a light on the hidden struggles that too often go unnoticed.

Together we are more than just survivors; we are agents of change and catalysts for a brighter future. As our organisation grows, I am reminded of the power of small habits to yield profound impact. Together we can harness the power of storytelling to create a world where every voice is heard, every story is valued and every woman is empowered to live her truth. Wherever you are in the world, whatever your story, I hope you have the courage to share it.

Whilst I no longer write the blog I began all those years ago, I still love to write. I am currently working on a book about single mothers in my community. My daughter enjoys writing too. It brings me much pleasure to see her writing from a place of joy and happiness, not from loneliness as I did when I was her age. I've managed to build a respectable relationship with my ex's family, and my daughter enjoys the support of both her mother, father and extended family. I hope as she gets older, she has the opportunity to travel, find a group of supportive females and to know her own value.

To find out more about Hong's work visit: *catalystforchangevietnam.com.*

Epilogue

Owning our Pivotal Moments

By Fleur Chambers

Have you realised the secret of this book yet? It is not just a book about habits; it is a book about how we create meaning in, and of, our lives.

There is something I'd like you to know about every courageous writer who contributed to this anthology: sharing their (very personal) stories did not always come easily. Each of these writers went through a personal journey to get their perspective on the page. They faced self-doubt and creativity blocks. They challenged their egos and danced with vulnerability in order to share a part of themselves which, in many cases, they'd never talked about publicly. For that, I want to applaud them.

I didn't just ask these authors to write about a habit, I challenged them to share a story of inner transformation and the reason they were called to transform. For many of the writers, the process was both revealing and healing.

Interestingly, as we worked together, they called on their habits to soothe themselves during the roller-coaster of writing, especially during the editing process. Together, we meditated on receiving feedback, identifying the 'real' story, and how to write in a way that allows the reader to see themselves. We leaned into the sense of collaboration and community that arises when people come together to create a book.

As the editor of this book, Amy Molloy says: 'It's not just about what you write, it's about how you feel as you write it.' I'd like to add, it's also about normalising the highs and lows that come with any creative process and with sharing yourself more deeply.

Writing and sharing our story is a powerful way to create meaning. Our stories speak to a moment in time whilst simultaneously drawing upon all the moments that have come before. And, in writing them, we send a GPS to the universe, or to life, that we are here, owning our pivotal moments, our actions and our life choices.

We get to interpret the events of our lives, to choose how and why we connect the dots of our experiences. We get to speak of both pain and joy from a place of authenticity, honesty and empowerment. Over seventeen stories, we have witnessed many ways to create meaning, from meditation that connected people to some well-earned forgiveness, to time spent on or in the ocean that consolidated friendships, and poetry and pool swimming as gentle reminders that the medical model isn't the only way to respond to mental, emotional and physical pain.

If you wrote your story, what themes would act as the thread that weaved your days, months and years together: forgiveness, compassion, courage, adventure, humour, honesty, resilience? You don't need to have gone through the *Meditate, Write, Celebrate* experience to commit to understanding yourself and your life more deeply. You can begin by asking yourself these questions.

- What did you enjoy from your childhood and how can you weave the energy or feelings that underpin this into your adult life?
- Is there something that you do now that allows you to connect with your younger self? How can you use this habit, hobby or experience as a way to feel more compassionate, gentle or forgiving towards your younger self?
- Is there a habit that you could expand upon so that it transforms into an act of service or a way to contribute to the world?
- How could you use your habits or hobbies to foster more meaningful connections with family, friends, colleagues or strangers?
- Is there something in your life that you could allow to hold greater meaning, helping you connect with the memory of your parents, grandparents or lineage?
- How could you make your everyday habits like cooking, gardening or walking the dog feel more sacred or meaningful?
- How could you use your habits to explore the mind-body connection as you respond to experiences like chronic pain, neurodivergence, aging, illness or mental health challenges?
- How could you incorporate more sunrises and sunsets into your weeks?

If you are keen to explore some new habits or ways of interacting with the world, turn the page for our *Fourteen-Day North Star Habit Challenge*. Inspired by our writers, these simple prompts will encourage you to get out of your comfort zone and shake up your daily routine with joy and ease. Who knows, you might even discover a new habit or hobby that feels like a missing piece to the puzzle that is you.

Thanks for being part of this celebration of simple habits and the profound impact they can have on our lives. If you feel inspired to share your North Star habits with us, or to be part of the next *Meditate, Write, Celebrate*, please get in touch at *thehappyhabit.com.au*. Together, let's share our stories and offer one another the gift of feeling seen and heard.

Fourteen-Day North Star Habit Challenge

Day One: Talk to a stranger. Help someone feel good. Offer a compliment or have a laugh. Allow the sense of connection to land in your body and remind you that we are more the same than different.

Day Two: Make a hearty soup. Don't forget to put on an uplifting playlist and sing your heart out as you do it. Let this be an act of self-care and compassion.

Day Three: Switch up your walking habits. Go somewhere new, don't take your phone. Focus on the journey not the destination. Cultivate curiosity. Let the sights, sounds and the season fill you with awe and wonder.

Day Four: Try 'free writing'. Set a timer for five minutes and write down your thoughts, feelings or memories in a journal or notebook –

don't overthink it, just see what comes up.

Day Five: Sit in meditation for ten minutes. Imagine you are breathing in and out of your heart. Notice emotions. Allow them to come and go like clouds in the sky. Be curious about what is there, beneath the surface of your busy mind.

Day Six: Go for a cold-water swim or have a cold shower. Challenge yourself. Be with the discomfort. Speak to your body and remind it, *There is no need to panic. You are safe, it's just sensation. All is well.*

Day Seven: Move from fear to love. Close your eyes and notice any fear that's present in your body, mind or heart. Ask yourself, *What would love look and feel like right now?* Take a step towards love.

Day Eight: Sit at your window. Set a timer for five minutes and take in the nature outside (even if you live in a city – there's still nature). What can you notice about your natural surroundings that you've never noticed before; what can it teach you about your place in the world?

Day Nine: Catch a sunrise or sunset. Go for the one you don't usually see. For an added dopamine boost, rope in some friends and include some movement. Why not meet a friend as the sun comes up over the weekend?

Day Ten: Embrace multiple passions. Is there a habit or hobby you've forgotten or neglected because you've been solely focused on one thing? How can you mix up your routine today and embrace a multi-passioned life?

Day Eleven: Learn from your ancestors. Think about a wise relative in your life – maybe it's a grandmother, a great-aunt or a loving elder who was not related to you by blood. What advice would they give you today; what small step would they tell you to take to change your outlook and your energy?

Day Twelve: Make a splash. Switch up your exercise routine and head for a swim, whether it's in your local pool or the ocean. Welcome a feeling of flow into your body. How does being in the water make you feel?

Day Thirteen: Speak to a higher being. You don't have to be 'spiritual' to ask for guidance outside yourself. Send a question out to the moon, the trees or the sky – and see what answer comes back to you.

Day Fourteen: Stop, look and listen. Break the cycle of forward momentum by pausing a few times today and noticing sensations in your body, thoughts in your mind and emotions within your heart. What intelligence did you access? From this place of grounded awareness, choose your next move.

If you share your North Star habits on social media, make sure you tag us @thehappyhabitwithfleurchambers. Let's continue the ripple of hope and healing.

References

Aron, E. 2020, *The Highly Sensitive Person: How to Thrive When the World Overwhelms You.* New York, Three Rivers Press.

Balasubramanian, V. 2021, Brain Power. *Biological Sciences.* FF 118(32). https://doi.org/10.1073/pnas.2107022118

Benson, L. 2022, *Where Have I Been All My Life?: How I Finally Grew Up After a Life of Putting Up, Giving Up and Shutting Up.* KMD Books.

Clear, J. 2018, *Atomic Habits: An Easy and Proven Way to Build Good Habits and Break Bad Ones.* New York, Avery.

Gordon, A. and Ziv, A. 2021, *The Way Out: A Revolutionary, Scientifically Proven Approach to Healing Chronic Pain* . New York, Avery.

Grahame, K. 2008, *The Wind in the Willow*. Puffin Modern Classics

Madson, P. 2005, *Improv Wisdom: Don't Prepare, Just Show Up*. New York, Crown.

Milkman, K. 2022, *How to Change: The Science of Getting from Where You Are to Where You Want to Be*. New York, Portfolio/Penguin.

Neff, K. 2011, *Self-Compassion: The proven power of being kind to yourself*. New York, Harper Collins.

Nichols, W. 2015, *Blue Mind: The Surprising Science That Shows How Being near, in, on, or under Water Can Make You Happier, Healthier, More Connected and Better at What You Do*. New York, Little, Brown and Company.

Rinpoche, S. 2017, *The Tibetan Book of Living and Dying*. London, Rider.

Thaler, R. H. and Sunstein, C. R. 2008, *Nudge: Improving Decisions About Health, Wealth, and Happiness*. Yale University Press.

Wave, B. 2019, *The Top Five Regrets of the Dying: A Life Transformed by the Dearly Departing*. Hay House.

Wikipedia contributors. 2024, Bipolar II disorder. In: Wikipedia, *The Free Encyclopedia*. https://en.wikipedia.org/w/index.php?title=Bipolar_II_disorder&oldid=1235283020

Wikipedia contributors. 2024, Hypomania. In: Wikipedia, *The Free Encyclopedia*. https://en.wikipedia.org/w/index.php?title=Hypomania&oldid=1234060174

Winton, T. 2009, *Breath*. Camberwell, Penguin Books.

Acknowledgements

I'll keep these short and sweet.

Heartfelt gratitude to each of the contributing authors. As I mentioned in the epilogue, identifying and sharing your story requires self-awareness, courage and clarity. Thanks for showing up to every Zoom call, for listening to one another so beautifully, for diving deep into meditation and your past. Thanks for sharing your hard-earnt lessons and for trusting me. Your stories fit neatly on the page for the enjoyment of the reader, but only because of your willingness to get messy along the way.

Just as I have held space for these authors to move through their creative process, three awesome and incredibly different women have held space for me – a beautiful reminder that giving and receiving come from the same place of generosity and collaborative spirit.

To Amy Molloy, for providing the foreword and the 'big' edit for each of these stories. Your ability to pack a punch with few words, to identify the themes that connect both writer and reader and your genuine delight in people's inner and outer worlds make you an integral

ACKNOWLEDGEMENTS

part of the books I create. You are incredibly generous when you edit, you help people share from a place of safety and you are normalising our human vulnerabilities one story at a time.

To Jacqui Lewis, my mentor, for breaking all the 'meditation teacher' rules and for reminding me that being unapologetically ourselves is the best strategy for life. Thanks for showing me how to be gentle, compassionate, funny, clever, wise, wacky and humble all at once.

To Karen McDermott, my publisher, for saying 'yes' to every book idea I propose and for continuing to hint at how I would enjoy a project like this until I finally listened. You were right, I love helping other people share their stories.

Thank you, Rick Hanson, for endorsing and sharing my work, and for introducing me to the concept of North Star habits, values, attitudes and ways of being in the world.

A big thanks to my four boys and my dog, Lucky, for making home a place I love to be.

And finally, much gratitude to you, for reading this book, for seeing yourself in these chapters, for connecting with our shared humanity, and for celebrating the power of storytelling. May you follow your own North Star.

Curator – Fleur Chambers

Fleur Chambers is a multi-award-winning meditation teacher, Creator of *The Happy Habit* app, bestselling author of *Ten Pathways* and *Wholehearted Confidence* and philanthropist. Through her guided meditations, courses and books, Fleur is helping people all around the world say *yes* to their entire lives, even the challenges and difficulties.

With proceeds from *The Happy Habit* funding grassroots projects in some of the poorest communities around the world, Fleur is using meditation, self-enquiry and story as tools for social change. To date, *The Happy Habit* has provided sixty thousand people with access to a lifetime's clean drinking water.

Often referred to by her students as gentle, curious and warm-hearted, Fleur reminds us that there is strength in softness and that we are safe to be ourselves.